MW00880529

FOLLOWING JESUS
The Way, The Truth, and The Life

by
Howard Storm

PUBLISHED BY
KRATOS PUBLISHERS

ENCOUNTERING JESUS:
THE WAY, THE TRUTH, AND THE LIFE

Copyright © 2024 by Howard Storm

Published by: Kratos Publisher

All rights reserved under international copyright law. No part of this book may be reproduced without permission in writing from the copyright owner, except by a reviewer, who may quote brief passages in review.

Scripture quotations are from:

KJ21
21st Century King James Version, Copyright © 1994 by Deuel Enterprises, Inc.

NIV
Holy Bible, New International Version®, NIV® Copyright ©1973, 1978, 1984, 2011 by Biblica, Inc.® Used by permission. All rights reserved worldwide.

NRSVA
New Revised Standard Version Bible: Anglicised Edition, copyright © 1989, 1995 the Division of Christian Education of the National Council of the Churches of Christ in the United States of America. Used by permission. All rights reserved.

NMB
New Matthew Bible, Copyright © 2016 by Ruth Magnusson (Davis). Includes emendations to February 2022. All rights reserved.

Endorsements

Having clinically died and met the One who loves us passionately, Howard has dedicated his life to loving and serving Jesus. Through his decades of study, reflection, and pastoral work, Howard shares the practical way to love and follow Jesus wholeheartedly, and his message is one of hope and encouragement for all who seek a deeper connection with God.

— John Burke, author of the New York Times bestseller Imagine Heaven.

Howard Storm has experienced some unimaginable things. He has personally experienced a reality that we have all only gotten very small doses of; in the most gruesome of horror films that Hollywood has dreamed up. The real thing is far more terrifying than even the most depraved Hollywood minds can imagine... and Howard went through it, beyond the threshold of death itself, and was sent back to this earth-bound reality, directly from Jesus Christ; in order to deliver the message of the pure unconditional "agape" love, that God has for each and every one of us.

I have followed Howard for decades, and this is because his story is true and authentic. As Howard will tell you, the living nightmare he experienced was a divine blessing from Jesus, a merciful act of desperation from a God who loves us beyond measure. Howard is a living testimony to God's Divine mercy upon us all and a stark warning that there are eternal repercussions to the choices that we all make in our lives. Choose wisely and I encourage anyone to listen to Howard's words. The light of Jesus shines directly on this man. We all need to pay close attention to what he has to say and follow Jesus through the revelation of Howard's unique experiences.

— Brian Rayner, founder of JTB Online LLC.

Contents

Introduction

"Who are we? Where are we going? Where have we been?"

These questions are the title of a large painting by Paul Gaugin that hangs in the Museum of Fine Arts in Boston, Massachusetts. The title may be slightly incorrect, but that is how I remember it from my childhood. This painting captured my attention, my mind, and my heart; I spent many visits staring at this masterpiece.

On the left, Gaugin, the artist, painted a young woman holding a baby. In the centre, he pictured a beautiful, mature woman, and on the right-hand side, he showed us a striking old woman. The artist's exotic colors, the tropical plants, and the Tahitian people fascinated me. Did Gaugin know the answer to the big mysteries of life? I wondered and wondered for all of my early life. Is this it? You're born, you live your life (such as it is), and then you die?

From my teenage years onwards, my friends and family lived more or less for today and had no interest in God or the afterlife. We didn't go to church and held in contempt those who were religious. The churchgoers were delusional since they couldn't accept the reality of a materialistic universe with nothing beyond that.

These delusional churchgoers supposedly make up the majority of the population of the United States. However, referring to oneself as a Christian, Jew, or Muslim doesn't mean one takes God seriously. In surveys, people often say they believe in God, but they don't live that way. If one believed in God, wouldn't they take that seriously? In 1985, I died and had an intense near-death experience. I learned to take God and Jesus very seriously. This experience was transformative and changed my life in every way possible. My book, 'My Descent into Death', is about my near-death experience and how it transformed me.

That is the focus of this book: Taking God seriously. What do we do with that responsibility? This is the critical decision, the important crossroad in our lives. What are the obligations of faith? What are we going to change, and are there sacrifices involved? Hopefully, we deeply considered these questions when we chose a career, made decisions about marrying, and decided whether to start a family, as well as everything else important to us in our lives. Hopefully, we spent much time pondering these questions in a variety of ways. There is nothing in life more important than these questions.

That is the general outline of this book. More specifically, where is this going? When you travel, it is very good to have a map, whether printed on paper or on a GPS screen. How frustrating and sometimes frightening it is to be lost. I know a large number of people who have had that experience, and what a relief it is to have a map to reorient and redirect ourselves! There are recreational times when we may walk or drive without any particular goal except for adventure, but we typically do this when we know a way out or back. Perhaps one could even live this way, but most people need and want a sense of security and control of knowing where they are and where they are going.

This book is a map based on thousands of years of mapmaking. Let me share the collective wisdom, experience, and understanding of the map. Let me, to the best of my ability, articulate and reveal the truth of this journey of life. Billions of people have used this map for over two thousand years. The map is the Christian faith, and that faith is shown to us through the Bible, the church, and the Holy Spirit. The Holy Spirit is our constant and internal guide on this journey. This abiding Spirit is also known as the Spirit of Christ. Christ is always with us and will guide us if we pay attention.

Please read everything written in this book critically. Question everything you do not agree with or understand differently. Critical thinking is the only way to discern the probability between truth, lies, and deception. Science is based on evidence that confirms the truth of an idea or proves it to be false. It is the intention of this book to present the truth that can be confirmed historically, experientially, and by consensus of respected authorities on the particular subject. The truth I know is that God is love. Discuss this guide with a priest or a pastor.

In contemporary society, we are under siege by scams, con artists, and frauds. It is a daily struggle to know who or what to trust and believe. It is often bewildering and maddening. To survive by rational and evidence-based decision-making requires research and doing the 'work'. What we do with our life is a decision, and one actually based on the choices we make every moment of our life. Be exceedingly careful whom you believe. Look at their credentials, look at the body of their work, and compare these to the Gospels.

May the content of this book be a guide to you, the reader, so that you will be filled with "love, joy, peace, patience, kindness, generosity, faithfulness, gentleness, and self-control." *(Galatians 5:22-23 [NRSVA]).* These are the fruits of the Spirit, which is the indwelling Spirit of Jesus Christ, and the destination of this journey. You will receive these gifts on your journey. Jesus will be with you along the way, and you will have His joy.

We will be discussing the scientific reliability of the scriptures, their sources, and their unique messages. We will also look at the historical documents of the Christian testaments and how they compare with other historical documents. You will find quotes from the scriptures and quotes from Jesus that I, the author, received in my experience with Him. There has been nothing directly received from Jesus that contradicts Jesus as He is revealed in the Gospels. My understanding of scripture, theology, and Christian faith has been wonderfully increased and expanded by my education at the United Theological Seminary and the many scholars I have read over the past decades. However, the major revelation of God, the Son of God, and the Holy Spirit have been a personal experience through listening to mature Christian friends, and the guidance of the Holy Spirit.

God has graciously given me love, hope, and faith, which is not a reward for anything I have done. Rather, these graces are a form of love which our Creator desires to give to anyone who seeks them - these good gifts.

"Ask, and it will be given you; search, and you will find; knock, and the door will be opened for you."

Matthew 7:7 [NRSVA]

Is this a promise from Christ Jesus? Yes, it is a promise, and it is true. Please appreciate that some of these "good gifts" may take time, and we get these graces when we are ready to receive them.

No good parent gives a young child an automobile until they are ready. God, our Creator, is better and wiser than the best human parent, and God has blessed us humans with a vast range of good gifts.

Of great importance is the gift of free will, which is the ability to decide between good and evil or, in other words, right and wrong. We have the freedom to make choices, and that is the very definition of freedom. We are constantly struggling with making the choice which is consistent with our understanding of God. This brings us to the critical question: Who is our God? Christians believe that Jesus Christ was fully human and fully God. This foundational understanding of Christians will be explored further in this book. God is and was a mystery, but He has chosen to reveal His true self for thousands of years to every tribe and nation. Humans have repeatedly misused, abused, and exploited these revelations for the purposes of control, domination, and self-rewards. In Christianity, one of the fundamental truths is that Jesus Christ is the full, perfect, and complete revelation of God. This revelation of God is explicit in the Gospels of Matthew, Mark, Luke, and John. Everything in the Old Testament and the New Testament must be measured by the standard of Jesus. Over two thousand years, Jesus has drawn billions of people to follow Him. Many of these followers have sacrificed everything to follow him.

To really know Jesus is to love him and to give Him your best in love.

I repeat, sadly, humankind has perverted the revelation of God more often than not and continues to do so to this day. There would be no need for a book such as this if it were otherwise.

"You will know them by their fruits."

Matthew 7:16 [NRSVA]

You can take this to the bank. Another way of saying the same thing is to "consider the source." That is what draws billions of people to Jesus because His life, works, and words are far superior to any being who has ever lived on this planet. This is the person of Jesus revealed in the Gospels.

That is the ultimate goal, which is to try our best to follow the example Jesus Christ lived and taught by word and deed. God knows we try and fail, and then we try and fail again and again. God knows, and He forgives us when we take it to Him in heartfelt confession and repentance. We stumble up the mountain of sanctification, each on our own unique journey. This is the struggle of life in this world that everyone lives in. Humankind was created to live in harmony with God, our Father, with every other person, with our brothers and sisters, and with the Earth. In my near-death experience, Jesus took me to and showed me this world of the future Heaven on Earth. I have described this in my book 'My Descent into Death'. Our future is beautiful and peaceful beyond anything we have imagined. Embracing God's love is what will bring this about.

What if we tried this by offering support to one another? I will give you a hand up, and you give me a hand up. Does that sound like a plan? We might even trust one another enough to call each other brother and sister. Imagine that we are like family, loving and caring for each other, thus getting to resemble paradise on earth. What a stretch of the imagination. Does this make one recall the promises of God in the Scriptures? "Thy kingdom come on earth, as it is in heaven." Where have we heard this before? What do you think? Do you have a better plan? If you have a better plan, please let me know so I can join you. Until then, I am following Jesus. Our standard for discussing what is truly God's will and what is mistakenly human will attributed to who God is. How is this consistent with Jesus Christ, the perfect revelation of God? The Old and New Testaments are a historical record of human history and the evolving relationship with God over a period of thousands of years. Search for the golden nuggets in the Bible and understand where the writer has missed the mark.

I hope to see you alongside me as we climb the mountains and walk through the valleys on the adventure called 'Life'.

The Creator and The Creature

1

The Creator and The Creature

"So God created humankind in his image, in the image of God he created them; male and female he created them. God blessed them, and God said to them, 'Be fruitful and multiply, and fill the earth and subdue it; and have dominion over the fish of the sea and over the birds of the air and over every living thing that moves upon the earth'."

Genesis 1:27-28 [NRSVA]

The first thing I was taught at the United Theological Seminary in Dayton, Ohio, is that we humans are incapable of understanding God. For many weeks, I wondered why this is so. I finally realized that God is so vastly greater than us as humans. The Divine One is a mystery, but He has chosen to be revealed to an extent that we can comprehend. This gift of God is called revelation. From the beginning of history, there are records of people who claim they have had these revelations. The scriptures are full of these revelations of God, but they are often contradictory, which makes it difficult to know which are reliable and which are mistaken. Moreover, what was the original revelation and how has it been changed over time?

The Creator and The Creature

Here is an obvious example: Did God command the Jewish followers to slaughter all the men, women, and children of the towns they captured? This is contradictory to the commandment God gave Moses: "Thou shalt not kill." These cannot both be true. How is one to know what is a true revelation of God and what is not true? The Bible says, "God is love." *(John 4:8 [NRSVA])*. Does a loving God command the slaughter of whole towns, including every man, woman, and child? Is this not an irreconcilable contradiction to a loving God?

The Bible was written by those who claimed to be inspired by God. One has to believe that some testimonies were more inspired than others. Christians believe the Gospels of Matthew, Mark, Luke, and John are fully inspired, and so are most of the epistles (letters). Christians believe there are many inspired testimonies in the Hebrew Testament, but that some parts are not inspired. Some of the testimonies in Hebrew scripture show the worst of human character and attribute it to God.

Some Christians say what was written before Jesus Christ is no longer relevant, but there is a serious problem with this reasoning. Jesus Christ is the perfect revelation of God, not just when he lived for thirty years on this Earth two thousand years ago. Jesus Christ existed as a persona of God from the beginning of time. The Christ is the divine activity of God. The Christ is the creative activity that made the world described in the book of Genesis. Jesus Christ is not something created. Jesus Christ is part of the One God. Christians are monotheists and thus do not believe in three gods. Jesus showed me during my near-death experience some of His life where he walked the earth. Some of his life was filled with laughter with his disciples, and some of his life was filled with danger and suffering. He was amazing. He never lost his patience and self-control in everything he showed me. God is the same yesterday, today, and tomorrow.

This revelation was meant to change the world, and to an extent, it has. However, we haven't achieved Heaven on Earth yet. No one knows when that will occur, but Christians know that time is coming. We hope the Spirit of Christ will reign soon.

There is more than sufficient testimony in the Hebrew and Christian testimonies to know God as a God of love, justice, and mercy. Humans run amok, and God forgives and tries to set them on the right path. Frankly, the God revealed in the person of Jesus Christ is beyond human comprehension in love, forgiveness, kindness, truthfulness, humility, and all the virtues. (I will discuss self-sacrifice and suffering as the ultimate virtue in another chapter). God gave humans free will in the beginning and God respects our free will whatever we do. During my near-death experience, I asked Jesus why he didn't just write in the sky, "God is real." He said that the love of God is a free will choice and cannot be forced. Accepting and living with God is a choice we each make.

The big question is, "Who is your God?" Have you ever considered that your God is too small? If the love God has for you does not bring tears to your eyes out of gratitude, your God is too small. If you have no need to worship God, you are far from God. Knowing God means fully welcoming Him into your heart, mind, and soul.

Some consider all the beauty and good in the world and turn away from all the evil and ugliness that is around. You are what you focus on. God has created a good world full of contrast: Joy and sorrow, truth and lies, opportunities and obstacles, and good versus evil. We have the ability to choose what we participate in. This is the curriculum of life in the school of this existence on earth. We are created as children of God to make the right choices. If we try to make the right choices, we will go to Heaven and live in bliss forever. If we choose to ignore or be opposed to God, we will not go to Heaven. The alternative to Heaven is exceedingly horrible. This is not punishment; rather, it is for us to experience what we have inflicted on others whilst we were in the world. Possibly, this rehabilitation will change our character, and we will seek God with all our hearts, minds, and souls. In my near-death experience, I got to experience both Hell and Heaven. Hell is where we get to have all the hurt and pain that we have inflicted on people come right back at us. God gives everyone what is in their heart. In Heaven, our love for God is reciprocated with an even greater love, and we grow in that love.

God is a God of justice, love, mercy, and infinite wisdom. If there is any way to rehabilitate a person, God will find a way. If there is any way to refine a person, He will refine them and dispose of the dross.

"Who can endure the day of his coming, and who can stand when he appears? For he is like a refiner's fire."
Malachi 3:2 [NRSVA]

Some of us have been in the refiner's fire and prefer to never go there again. Perhaps this is why Alcoholics Anonymous says, 'Until a person has hit the gutter, they will not choose sobriety.' There is an easier path to God besides hitting rock-bottom, and that path is seriously seeking a relationship with God based on love while we have the opportunity to make a choice. It's your decision.

Religion is supposed to help people find their way to God. Oftentimes, it really does accomplish this. Unfortunately, there are many people who have rejected God because of the misuse and abuses of religion. All religions are human-made institutions that claim unique insight into God. Some have an abundance of inspiration, while others have little or none. Who is to judge which religion, church, or cult is credible? You are the one to make that decision. There is an old saying that 'if it walks like a duck, swims like a duck, and quacks like a duck, then it is probably a duck.' Let's put a specific church to that test. If it talks like Jesus, acts like Jesus, walks like Jesus, and loves like Jesus, then it is probably God's people knowing the true nature of Him as revealed by Jesus Christ.

Like many Christian bashers (which I was), my friends and I used to say that Christians were just a bunch of hypocrites. We imagined a big sign outside the church that stated, "If you have doubts, you are not welcome. If you have cheated on your spouse, you are not welcome. If you have ever lied, you are not welcome", et cetera. We imagined we would not be welcomed because we were guilty of many sins.

Another test of a specific religion, church, or group is: Do we see the love there or not? To be clear, we are talking about the act of love rather than the sentiment or emotion. We human beings tend to judge too quickly, and our judgments are based solely on our feelings; when we judge too quickly, we tend to make grave mistakes. We all want to be loved and accepted for who we are.

Obviously, one is not going to attend a church or group where you are not accepted for who you are. But (and here is the big caution), everyone wants to be loved and accepted, so we are inclined to be sold goods that are defective. A good church challenges us to follow Jesus more faithfully than what we are currently doing.

Knowing God, the Father, Son, and Holy Spirit takes one's entire existence, which includes this brief experience in the physical world and real life beyond time in Heaven. The process of having an intimate relationship with God begins in our early existence when we choose to receive God's love. All unconditional love originates from God, but it is too often not recognized. A life of gratitude acknowledging God's love in its myriad forms is not only an appropriate response, but it is also essential to growing an intimate love with God. Children are very trusting and loving, which makes them close to God. Unfortunately, this faith of children is frequently not nurtured or may even be disavowed.

Because gratitude in humility is absolutely critical to knowing God, the following are a few practical ways of giving thanksgiving in humility.

A beautiful way to give thanks to God is through worship. Corporate worship is often the purpose of the church and the primary work of a church service. Music has the power to transcend the ordinary and reach mystical states. The music may be classical, bluegrass, hymns, folk, or old-time; it does not matter as long as it touches your heart, soul, and mind. Music is just about perfect worship. One can also worship in this way alone, but corporate worship is often much more intense!

The first time I went to church in 1985, the ceiling was full of golden and radiant angels; hundreds of them smiling at us. I dropped to the floor and praised God. The ushers thought I had had a heart attack and gently lifted me into a pew. My wife was horrified, and I was in ecstasy. I have belonged to that church ever since.

Another way to express gratitude is by giving one's time, talents, and energies to the building of the Kingdom of God. On one hand, this could be through the ministries of a local church. On the other hand, it could be through community efforts not necessarily connected with a church. For example, community organizations like Alcoholics and Narcotics Anonymous, Al Anon, Habitat for Humanity, and others like them. These are just a few examples of community groups doing God's work. If one's passions are unique, like volunteering at a soup kitchen, hospital, museum, symphony or zoo, your passion moves you to build the Kingdom of God through your work and efforts; that is from your gratitude. There are times that this kind of work is difficult and exhausting, but giving the act of love back to God does not always have to be fun because it is always rewarding.

> **Here is a secret that you need to know: however much you give in love to God, He will reward you tenfold In much greater blessings.**

God gives good gifts, and it is important that we understand and seek them. If you are desiring a Cadillac or Mercedes Benz, you are setting yourself up for disappointment. If you are seeking love, hope, faith, etc. (how the "good gifts" are defined in the Bible), you will be blessed beyond your expectations. The best way to live is to expect nothing, want nothing, and anticipate nothing, and then you will find and receive, and the door will be opened. The point is simple: Let God be God.

Knowing God in truth is a lot about letting go of control and following in obedience to where you are led. Too many people go to church to be entertained or to have their egos inflated. Too many people perform acts of kindness to prove their superiority or assert their holiness. Too many people use religion to beat others into submission. These things are an offense to God.

God judges by the heart and not by appearances. We cannot deceive God. Our intention is supremely important when we are intimately in a relationship with Him. We must be scrupulous in our self-awareness by exploring our hearts, our intentions, and our purpose. Are we doing our best to please God or are we deceiving ourselves?

I would also caution against performing some act of love and expecting to feel a sense of satisfaction. It is not uncommon to feel guilty about this because it does feel good to please God, much in the way it would with your mother or father. Why would it not feel good to please your Creator? God is our Parent and is pleased even with the smallest action. Welcome joy into your heart because you did the right thing.

How many men and women have sacrificed their lives for the love of others?

"No one has greater love than this, to lay down one's life for one's friends."

John 15:13 [NRSVA]

These were not idle words that Jesus spoke. They were said a day before He was crucified. Jesus knew, and had known for a long time, what he was going to do. This was the plan of salvation for the world, of God sharing Heaven's great love. We are God's beloved children and God desires us to come to Heaven.

Men and women have been willingly sacrificing their lives all over the world for the sake of those they love and are rarely called 'heroes'. The millions of soldiers who have died in battle. Women and men who have sacrificed their lives for their families in thankless labor for the love of family. The woman who spent most of her time in a nursing home caring for her husband, who, after a severe stroke, lived in a vegetative state. After six years of nursing him every day, he died, and not long after, she died, exhausted. Men who worked themselves to death at lowly jobs to provide for their wives and children. These men and women may never have gotten much recognition, but God knows them and has welcomed them into their eternal home. These are the good and faithful servants.

What is your calling? Is there something you could do for those you love? What sacrifice would you be willing to make to do this? The world is full of these unsung heroes, and they are usually ignored. They never asked for glory; rather, they did this because of a conviction that this is what they needed to do. They will get their reward in eternal life. Our life in this world is just a moment compared to eternal life in Heaven. This is school, and the curriculum is love.

If you want to please God, use your life to care enough about someone and spend your time, talents, and resources helping them. Love the person you are with. Give your love away freely, without strings or expectations.

Give your love away wisely by the guidance of the Holy Spirit. Do not throw your love away where it is not welcomed. Jesus told his disciples to walk away and move on when they were not welcomed. There are ample people who will receive your love and care if you approach them in humility. There are also those who will take everything you offer and beg for more because they only want to use you for their gain. Without the guidance of the Holy Spirit, you will squander your compassion on wasted efforts.

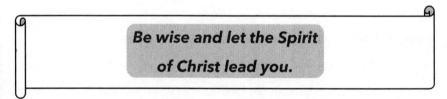

Be wise and let the Spirit of Christ lead you.

There is, and has been, only one Savior of the world, and it is not you. Start small with simple steps and discover how you are led to bigger challenges.

Is there a soup kitchen where you can volunteer one day a week? Is there a nursing home where you could visit a few lonely people? Do you have a well-behaved dog you could take to visit those who are alone? Your job is to love them, which means to listen to them. Your job is not to preach at them or to think you are going to change them. Your job is to give them unconditional love. Maybe you could say a prayer with them before you leave. People want to be heard, and your gift of love is to be present and to listen empathetically. Let them know they have been heard and that you accept them just as they are. Let the Spirit of Christ be in you and see the Spirit in them.

I love being a part of the church because we worship God through everything in the service. The church is made up of saints, sinners, and everything in between. I fit in perfectly, and you will fit in, too. It is such a joy to be part of a community of people seeking God. My brothers and sisters grow me in faith, love, and hope.

If you are blessed, they will share their joys and fears. If you are most blessed, they will share some of their deepest suffering and disappointments. You cannot fix these problems, but you can help make them more bearable by listening and letting them know they were heard without judgment. Yes, this can be exhausting and discouraging, but you will have a sense that you have helped heal a wounded heart. So many people are isolated, judged unworthy, depressed, and lost. By just being there and listening, we can bring a little of God's love, hope, and faith. This is pleasing to Him. With His help, you can do miracles.

The kingdom of Heaven is God's plan for humanity, the Earth, and the Universe. The Bible makes this explicit and indisputably clear. Perhaps one can disagree on the details of the kingdom on Earth as it is in Heaven, but those particulars will be relatively unimportant in relation to Heaven on Earth when it comes.

First let's describe our world as it exists today, beginning with the reality of it. 'Survival of the fittest' is the primary operating principle and has been from the beginning of life on Earth. The Christian commandment to "love one another" has been a minority proposition, and only rarely practiced. There are differences in nations on the degree of compassion shown to our brothers and sisters who are suffering; across most nations, there are vast inequities of wealth, health care, opportunities, education, and compassion.

The richest countries in the world have strong opposition to all attempts to equalize all the previously stated inequities. This stance is based on the notion of 'survival of the fittest' and is called Social Darwinism. This is simply described as it is: a dog-eat-dog world (which may be unfair to dogs). Craving for power, control, and amassing wealth dominate our culture because we think we are just animals. This is the lie of the evil one. The children of God were shown to me as kind, loving, and generous. Heaven is filled with love and joy. Life in Heaven is radically different from this world.

The poor are considered the most unfit, and the wealthy are deemed the fittest. This is presumed to be the way of nature and God's plan for humanity. However, this justification completely opposes the biblical revelation of God's plan and purpose for humankind. Remember, there are one billion people on this planet today who live on a dollar a day or less. We know all people have abilities, but social circumstances favor some and oppress others.

There are thousands of books written by scholars and politicians proposing ways to make this world a more compassionate and equitable place. We are not going down that road because it is outside the purpose of this book. You will come to your own conclusions, hopefully based on the Spirit of Christ.

> *Our purpose is knowing God and following the revelation of God found in the person of Jesus Christ.*

This is why we are born into this world. This is the work we have been given to do with our lives. There is nothing more important. Everything else besides living a God-inspired life is a distraction.

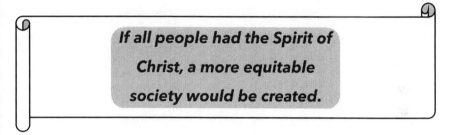

If all people had the Spirit of Christ, a more equitable society would be created.

The extremes of wealth, power, and oppression would end, and poverty would be eliminated.

So many things take us off course from the path we hope we are on. The path of righteousness is not self-righteousness. The right path is following God as revealed by the Son of God, the Messiah, the King of Kings, the Holy Spirit, Jesus of Nazareth, and our Savior. The best way (and probably the only way to know God) is to follow Jesus to the best of our ability in thought, word, and deed. This is the most challenging work in the world and the most rewarding. If you doubt this, you need to read the lives of women and men who have been called saints. These individuals have gone through trials that are beyond belief. One of the first persons called a saint is Paul, author of many of the New Testament letters. Paul writes:

"Five times I have received from the Jews the forty lashes minus one. Three times I was beaten by rods. Once I received a stoning. Three times I was shipwrecked; for a night and a day I was adrift at sea; on frequent journeys, in danger from rivers, danger from bandits, danger from my own people, danger from Gentiles, danger in the city, danger in the wilderness, danger at sea, danger from false brothers and sisters; in toil and hardship, through many a sleepless night, hungry and thirsty, often without food, cold and naked, and besides other things, I am under daily pressure because of my anxiety for all the churches."

2 Corinthians 11:24-28 [NRSVA]

This saint changed the world by planting churches all over the Roman Empire.

The apostle Paul's example is a challenge to our commitment to God. What are we complaining about? The purpose here is not to inflict guilt because we are so weak; the purpose is to encourage us to pursue the God who created us, loves us, and gives our lives meaning. Forget about the pie in the sky in the great by and by. Life is about this moment, today, where we are on the journey, trying to use every moment doing what we can to follow Christ Jesus' teaching and example. Use the Holy Spirit's guidance to share the love that God has given you in abundance, be the Spirit of Christ and seek that Spirit in everyone you meet. Change your little corner of the world.

Kindness is the beginning of life in the Spirit of Christ. This kindness is shown without judgment. Friend and foe are given this kindness. This begins by listening and not reacting too quickly. Treat everyone with respect and acknowledge their humanity. More importantly, search for the Christ in them and let them see the Christ in you.

To summarize what the Creator and the Creature is about:

> *"We know that all things work together for good for those who love God, who are called according to his purpose."*
>
> *Romans 8:28 [NRSVA]*

As many scholars have stated, the arc of history is upward. One has to step back to gain perspective to see this, but it is true. Humans are evolving slowly, but the pace of change is accelerating rapidly. The many challenges before us are daunting, but with the help of God, humanity will eventually thrive, and the world will be a better place.

"Thy kingdom come, thy will be done, on earth, as it is in Heaven."

Matthew 6:10 [NMB]

Therefore, the question for each one of us is: Are we going to be part of the problem or the solution? Living in neutrality is neither going forward nor backwards. In fact, it is part of the problem. Ignorance and indifference to the needs all around keep the status quo, but does anyone in the world really feel it is a perfect one, just as it is? Have we ever met such a contented person?

As I near the end of this chapter, I need to speak about risk assessment. The dangers of involvement are real because when you love, you become vulnerable, and you are at risk of being hurt emotionally. This is the downside to being loving, but if one is sharing the love of God as we are suggesting, there are ample opportunities to be knocked down and to love again and again.

If one is relying on their own human capacity for love, they will be defeated quickly.

Paul writes:

"For I am convinced that neither death, nor life, nor angels, nor rulers, nor things present, nor things to come, nor powers, nor height, nor depth, nor anything else in all creation will be able to separate us from the love of God in Christ Jesus our Lord."

Romans 8:38-39 [NRSVA]

To put this in plain vernacular: God's got this. If God calls you to do something, He will not abandon you in the process. No matter what the obstacles, if your task is truly from God, it will happen. You will be amazed by the grace you receive. When you hear the words "I once was blind but now I see," you will realise that you understand for the first time in your life.

How do you know if God really loves you? How do you know if you have a calling? How do you know it will work? The answer is strangely simple: pray. Talk to God. Too often, people state that they prayed and got no response. How is this possible? If God is omniscient, then how can God be absent or uninterested?

Consider that the failure to connect with God is the failure of the person and not the fault of God.

God is reaching out to us in subtle and not-so-subtle ways. Like the Beatles lyric, "All you need is love." How do we understand that? Prayerfully we can connect with God, but we have to have the Spirit of Christ to make the connection. Without the Spirit, we are lost.

Do we have any notion of how to listen for God to respond? The Holy Spirit abides in us, and that Spirit is trying to get our attention. We need to listen. Tune your heart and mind to the Spirit of Christ.

Let me share with you four simple ways to attune ourselves to an intimate relationship with God:

1. **Complete honesty and openness** are essential in a relationship with God. Tell Him everything, good and bad, that you have done in your life, including thought, word, and deed. Hold nothing back. God already knows you better than you know yourself. He wants to hear it from you. This will take a while. Read the Bible, especially Matthew, Mark, Luke, and John. Read only one short section and then reread it more slowly. You will come to know that God is speaking to you through those verses. Keep rereading until you understand what you never knew before. That is a sign God is speaking to you. The Spirit of God is within the words of the Bible.

> **The Bible is the only book that talks.**

2. **Speak about these things with someone who is a mature Christian.** God may well speak through another, and you will be surprised at the wisdom spoken. You would not ask an electrician to solve your plumbing problem, so ensure to speak about spiritual matters with a person who has a strong connection with God. Churches are the places to find such people. Not everyone who goes to church is a saint by any means, but there are saints in churches, and they do not promote themselves. You have to diligently hunt for them. These saintly people exist and are a treasure for you to find.

3. Lastly, **praying is a conversation with God that demands full attention** and is often based in silence. Have you ever experienced a rare and inspiring moment with someone where there were no words? Loving relationships frequently have those moments. Seek God's love and nothing else and you will be given what you need. You may not get what you thought you wanted, but you will get what you need. God loves you and wants to give you good gifts for your salvation.

As you seek an intimate relationship with God, it helps to remember these words from the Apostle Paul:

"All things work together for good to those who love God, who are called according to his purpose."

Romans 8:28 [NRSVA]

God is calling. Answer the door.

The Gospels

2

The Gospels

"But there are so many other things that Jesus did; if every one of these were written down, I suppose that the world itself could not contain the book that would be written."

John 21:25 [NRSVA]

The Gospels are the testimonies in the New Testament of Matthew, Mark, Luke, and John. The word Gospel means 'good news', and specifically, the life, words, and actions of Jesus Christ. These four books are the basis of the Christian faith. The Bible is full of golden nuggets, which are the inspired word of God. Our job is to find these inspired words of God and study them. The Bible will speak to you through the Holy Spirit if you go to it humbly and prayerfully. The Bible is the only talking book I know.

The Epistles were written by saints, and my personal hero is St. Paul. His writings are brilliant and loaded with God-breathed wisdom and truth. One of the reasons I love Paul is that he sometimes shows his human emotions, such as anger against his enemies. Paul was the greatest evangelist in the history of Christianity, and he was very human. How great it is to read his words, which reveal his human side.

The Gospels

The Hebrew Testament is not the same as the Gospels but provides important background to them. Christians search for passages in the Hebrew Testament that support the revelation of Jesus Christ described in the Gospels and Christians eject or ignore things that are inconsistent or contrary to the Gospels. Simply put, Christians understand the Gospels as the complete, perfect, and true revelation of God, Jesus, and the Holy Spirit. Everything else is imperfect and sometimes flawed, but useful.

To say that the Bible is the inspired word of God does not mean it is perfect. The entire Bible was a people's attempt to understand and interpret inspired experiences, but there are a few problems. Many of the Hebrew scriptures were written long after the revelations were received by the originator of the revelation. Secondly, these testimonies were rewritten generations after the source died and were added to and changed by the rewriter. Most importantly, the world, the culture, the circumstances, and society's view of the Israelites changed over thousands of years. The Hebrew literature was not assembled and edited until a council was assembled in the second century BC. How much scripture was rejected is not recorded, but it was probably a significant amount. Despite this change in language, however, the context and content of the Bible and its purpose remain true.

This process is also what happened with the collection of scriptures called the New Testament in the second century AD. We know of many scriptures that were excluded and some of the controversies around the selection process from Christians of that period.

It is important to remember that all inspired literature was recorded by humans and that humans are imperfect beings with their own agendas. That humanity, both good and bad, can be found in all Biblical literature. Anyone who studies Biblical literature is seeking the truth of God, but also must be aware of the author's translation and their intentions. Looking at Biblical literature passionately and honestly means seeking the inspired word of God and the author or translator critically.

> *Taking the Biblical literature literally without rational examination is not seeking the inspired word of God. Using the Bible literature if the spirit of Christ is absent is an empty endeavor.*

The Bible contains the inspired word of God, but it is only discovered through the power of the Holy Spirit's guidance. Everything in the Biblical testimonies must be rationally and spiritually investigated and understood. A superficial reading of the Bible does both the Word of God and the reader a great injustice.

Do your best to present yourself to God as one approved by him, a worker who has no need to be ashamed, rightly explaining the word of truth.

2 Timothy 2:15 [NRSVA]

The Biblical scriptures were predominantly written in Hebrew and Greek. Beginning with a rational appreciation of the Bible is knowing that, unfortunately, all English translations fail to perfectly translate Hebrew and Greek because it is impossible. The following are the reasons why and what one must do to find what the original authors wrote and were trying to communicate. When one researches a Hebrew or Greek word that is translated into English, there are often very important differences or variations. There are books written on this subject, but that is way beyond the purpose of this book. Buy a good, exhaustive concordance of the translation of the Bible you are using. If you take the Bible seriously, you will do the work to try to understand what is written in the original language.

The translators of the Bible have their own personal views, and those determine their translations. Their intentions are not deception; rather, they interpret to suit their personal theology and culture of the time they live in. These are not bad people; they are simply flawed human beings doing the best they can from their perspective. The reader will have a deeper understanding of the Word of God if they go beyond the surface of the translation, you are reading. Dig deeply into the Bible with the help of the Spirit.

One cannot find the truth of the Bible unless you have some understanding of the historical context that it was written in. Fundamentally, all Biblical literature was originated by an individual living in a very specific time and place. What is the historical context of the author and what were their hopes, fears, and beliefs in God? Did this author live in such a dangerous time and place that their hope was in a violent and ruthless God whose favor would ensure their survival? Did the author of the testimony struggle with a revelation of God such that they could barely explain it? **In a culture where women had no rights and were treated as property, how did these authors portray women and their relationships to men?**

The important understanding of context is essential to knowing the inspired Word of God in every piece of the Bible. Keep in mind an ancient author trying to convey a revelation of God to an audience thousands of years ago. Only if one does the work can one begin to know what God is saying.

The Bible is the most published book in the world and the selling of Bibles is a huge business. Go to any bookstore and see all the different Bibles for sale. Publishers are constantly coming out with new translations in new and attractive forms. The really big editions that weigh ten pounds or more are getting very expensive, so we find fewer notes and commentaries included in the cheaper Bibles. If you want help to understand the book of the Bible you are interested in, you must buy a commentary, and even better, buy a few different commentaries by different authors. One can also find many commentaries on the internet, and they are free. Many different translations of the Bible are also available on the internet for free. There is no excuse to be ignorant since more than you can possibly learn is freely available on the internet. What do you want to know about the Bible? The resources are readily available and the internet costs nothing to use. If you are serious about understanding what the Bible teaches, you will do the work. Jesus told me that there is no conflict between scientific truth and biblical truth. They are just two different ways of looking at and understanding the world.

If you really want to have fun learning the Word of God, join a Bible study. Bible studies are free and plentiful online. Most churches sponsor Bible studies and you do not have to join the church to attend. Any respectable person would welcome a new person to attend a Bible study group. One of the great advantages is that you get to meet many good people and have the opportunity to make new friends. The best incentive to be part of the Bible study is learning through discussion what insights others are getting from reading, studying, and thinking about the Bible. It is amazing how God works in Bible studies to develop our wisdom, guided by the Holy Spirit.

If the group is focused on Jesus Christ and the love of God, you are in the right group. If the group is centered on hate, exclusivity, and fear, then you need to leave that group and never go back.

Trust your heart to find the love of God in the good Bible study. You will be blessed.

The most important way to know God is by the power of the Holy Spirit. To open oneself to being guided by the Spirit, one must pray for that guidance. Without the intercession of the Spirit of God, you are going nowhere in your search for Him. This prayer starts with humility before a mighty and mysterious God. We are little children before the creator of the universe.

> **The Good News is that God wants to love us and wants us to have a loving relationship with His children .Jesus said "Let the little children come to me and do not stop them, for it is to such as these that the kingdom of God belongs."**
>
> Mark 10:14 [NRSVA]

Prayerfully approach the Holy Scriptures with all the innocence and trust of a little child and let the inspired Word of God speak to you. Be prepared to be surprised. You will always learn something new and wonderful. There is an old saying that 'the way to eat an elephant is in small bites, one at a time'.

The Gospels are the place to begin reading and understanding the Bible. They give us a complete and unvarnished depiction of God as He was incarnated in the person of Jesus Christ.

Evaluate everything you read in the Bible by the Spirit of Christ, the historical Jesus of Nazareth, and the testimony of those who Knew Him as written in the Gospels.

What the Gospels state are totally trustworthy and give us the complete revelation of God. If and when you really, really know Jesus, you are home. Home is where you are truly known, loved as you are, and completely forgiven. Home is where you are safe and appreciated. Home is where you belong and where you are going. Home is everything you hoped for and never found in your life. Home is God embracing you in a love beyond words that you could never have imagined. The Gospels will take you there. You are fully known and appreciated in God's home.

After you really know Jesus, the authors of the Epistles will make sense and you will know what the authors of the Hebrew Testament were seeking, finding, and occasionally missing.

The Gospels

How do you know the Gospel writers got it right? **We know the Gospels were written within the lifetime of those who lived with and knew Jesus.** There are some variations in what the Gospel writers put down, but they are all doing their best to describe the same Jesus.

Each of the Gospel writers had their own point of view, and one can know something about them from what they want to emphasize. However, the variations in the narratives are insignificant and do not detract from the truth of the revelation of God fully in human form. The four Gospel writers simply recorded the life and work of Jesus on earth, as best they could.

The Gospels were written by men who had direct knowledge from their experience of Jesus and wanted to share this life changing information with the world. The disciples and Jesus' many followers didn't profit by this work. They all sacrificed and suffered terribly for their dedication and love of Jesus.

There have been many who have tried to discredit the Gospel writers. They have profited from their efforts, but what else did they hope to gain? Why does a person try to discredit God? What motivation is there behind the demeaning of the Savior of the World and attacking the witness of his followers? One is forced to question the critic's motivation of those who seek to undermine the Christian faith. These critics are not trustworthy.

Archaeologists have searched and searched for evidence of the Gospels' authenticity. A few decades ago, it was a commonly held belief among scholars that there was no proof of Pontius Pilate being governor of Israel. When excavations began in Caesarea, Israel, which was Pontius Pilate's headquarters, a carved stone that carried the inscription 'Pontius Pilate, Governor' was unearthed. That settled that controversy. We will likely never find the Gospels carved in stone, but there have been fragments of the Gospels found, and some have been dated back to the first century. Some of the most convincing evidence for the early authorship and authenticity of the Gospels is a quotation from them found in the writings of the very earliest church fathers. These quotes from the first and second centuries are proof that the Biblical literature which is the basis for the Christian faith was available from the earliest beginnings.

Let me give you an example of how one church building was replaced by another, and a piece of information affirmed a Christian truth. During the early period of Christianity, a church was built in Nazareth. This is the town where Jesus grew up. This church was destroyed by the enemies of Christianity during the Byzantine era. Hundreds of years later, the Crusaders recaptured the area and built another Christian church on the same spot in Nazareth. After the church was completed, these Crusaders then excavated a nearby small house of stone. During the excavation, these Crusaders found an inscription on one of the walls of the house. It read "Home of Mary, the Mother of God."   There are countless proofs of the existence of Jesus and His life. One can investigate them, or one can dismiss them. Anything can be contradicted by anybody. We have the freedom to choose what is true and what is false. What are you seeking?

When one considers the extreme hardship of the early church to exist and increase throughout the Roman empire, which did everything in its empirical power to suppress Christianity, it is a miracle that Christianity not only survived but spread rapidly. Consider a world where most of the travel was by foot or sailboat. There was no postal service and paper was very expensive. Communications took weeks and months, and the Christians were being hunted. How did Christianity, based on the Gospels, become the religion of the Roman Empire in three hundred years when Emperor Constantine established it, ending the slaughter of Christians? It is miraculous that it survived and thrived through three centuries of brutal oppression.

The reality is that tens of thousands of women and men braved the penalty of torture and death to tell the Gospel stories of Jesus and share their manuscripts. Through their courage and devotion, Christianity conquered the biggest and one of the most exceedingly violent empires the world has ever known. Back then, there were dozens of competing religions and thousands of prospering temples and shrines catering to every desire of the pagan world. Christianity taught a morality that was unlike anything in the Roman world. The Roman Empire was based on cruelty and greed. They conquered people to loot their wealth and to enslave them. Their primary entertainment was in the coliseum, where men, women, and children were fed to wild animals. People were executed by the tens of thousands.

Christianity has a strict code of morality, but it has never been close to the brutality of Rome. The more Christian people become, the less likely they are to be cruel. Jesus' standards are totally loving and not punitive. What was the attraction of faith in Jesus Christ? The only possible explanation is that it had a powerful appeal to many people. I suggest to you that the power behind that appeal was the Holy Spirit, the Spirit of God, revealed in the Spirit of Jesus Christ.

During the two-thousand-year history of Christianity, there have been countless thousands of martyrs, many of whom are hardly known. Were they all delusional or psychotic? From a Christian perspective, the answer is no. They were simply convinced of the proof of the Gospels. How many of us today have that kind of conviction that we would be willing to risk our lives for our faith? We do not know what we would do under the duress of torture and the threat of a horrible death. It is senseless to speculate, and by the grace of God, we will never have to face that challenge. **There is an old saying that 'the church was built on the blood of the martyrs'.** This is sadly true. They were not compelled by the government to sacrifice their lives. They usually lost wealth, property, prestige, power, and family. How can this kind of dedication to an idea be explained? Their amazing example of faith in Jesus Christ led so many to crave that kind of courage and belief. There are individuals today living in that same faith.

There is power in the Gospels that radically changes lives. God is still very much active in the lives of millions of people all over the world. Curiously, there is vastly greater expansion of Christianity in less developed places in the world than in the developed world across Europe and America. **The Church is declining in the developed world and rapidly expanding in the less developed world.** The difference is obviously that the former has significantly greater wealth, and the latter has substantially less wealth.

The rise of materialism clearly diminishes the appeal of Christian values.

Focus on the acquisition of property, money, and the power to get more is emphatically contradicted by God's will in the Gospels. Consequently, the Gospels are radically opposed to that part of the culture of the developed world. This is a legitimate explanation of why the **Christian faith is in decline in the Western countries** of Europe and America**.**

In these areas (American and Europe), there are churches that have incorporated wealth and property into their theology, and this is known as the 'prosperity Gospel'. **There were (and are) churches that teach misogyny, racism, and homophobia in their messages**. These churches seem to be growing. Do you find any of these doctrines in the life, work, and teachings of Jesus in the Gospels? No! What you will find is quite the opposite. Appealing to hate, fear, and wealth have their appeal to some.

However, the Gospels depict a love so beyond our worldly experience that it is difficult to accept. Only with an indwelling Spirit of God can we begin to manage to live the life Jesus describes. More specifics of this life of following Jesus will be discussed further in this book. Reading the Gospels, when taken seriously, is very challenging to the mature Christian and ridiculous to the non-Christian. It is only by the grace of God that any of this makes sense.

The Gospels

Do you feel called by God to go deeper? Are you worried that you may have to change or give up something? Is it possible that the Gospels set a standard that is impossible to meet? The answer is yes and no. When an individual sincerely seeks God, they will get far more than they ever expected, but what they get will usually differ from their desires. As is said in Alcoholics Anonymous, 'let go and let God'. God has good things for you.

The Person of Jesus

3

The Person of Jesus

"I will baptize you with water; but he will baptize you with the Holy Spirit."

Mark 1:8 [NRSVA]

There are two sides to the person of Jesus: the fully human and the fully divine. If you find this hard to comprehend, welcome to the mystery of God. Christians are monotheists and believe there is only one God. They also believe that God has revealed Himself in three separate ways: God the Supreme Being, Christ, the creative activity of God, and the Spirit who indwells humankind if they choose it. This is the same as saying Father, Son, and Holy Ghost. In this chapter, we will be discussing the Christ who appeared to the world sometime around a few years before BCE and lived into his early thirties, when he was crucified by the Romans. This God wants to abide in us through the Holy Spirit.

Jesus is the best friend I know. He knows everything I have ever done and everything I have ever thought. He only wants the best for me, which is to become the child of God I was created to be. He has appeared to me on a few occasions, but more importantly, I have felt his presence and love when I needed it. To feel him close with his arm around me and pouring his love on me is the best thing I experience in life.

We know more about the person of Jesus Christ than any other figure because of the testimonies in the Gospels, and the millions of testimonies of millions of Christians over the last two thousand years. The person of Jesus is a revelation of God that lived as one of us two thousand years ago and who continues to reveal Himself today. There are hundreds of books, YouTube videos, and verbal testimonies speaking about encounters with Jesus.

Why one person has met Jesus and another person has not met Jesus is not known to us, but it is God's way and beyond anyone's understanding. Anyone can speculate about why God does what He does, but that is not worth much. God's ways are not our ways.

We do have the reported words of Jesus and his actions that tell us why he came into the world fully human. Also, there are the words of the earliest witnesses of Jesus as to why he came to us. In Paul's letter to the Philippian Church 2:5-11, we have what is considered to be the earliest formal creed of the Christian faith composed by the first generation of Christians.

Let the same mind be in you that was in Christ Jesus, who though he was in the form of God, did not regard equality with God as something to be exploited, but emptied himself, taking the form of a slave, being born in human likeness, and being found in human form, he humbled himself and became obedient to the point of death – even death on a cross.

Therefore, God also highly exalted him and gave him a name that is above every name, so that at the name of Jesus every knee should bend, in Heaven and on Earth and under the Earth, and that every tongue should confess that Jesus Christ is Lord to the glory of God the Father.

Philippians 2:5-11 [NRSVA]

Let's break this down to glean what this tells us about the person of Jesus. First, we are asked, "to have the same mind that was in Christ Jesus." Jesus taught, healed, travelled, did miracles, suffered, died, and rose from death in the presence of many persons. He did these things so that we would understand and know God completely according to our ability to grasp these things. This is an "amazing grace," about which I am intentionally referencing a popular song which expresses these things so beautifully. Previously God has been revealing His will universally to all people, and they have typically been misusing and abusing these revelations with only some exceptions. God gave the world a revelation that is difficult to misinterpret in Jesus Christ.

"For God so loved the world that he gave his only Son, so that everyone who believes in him may not perish but may have eternal life."

John 3:16 [NRSVA]

This verse is so often quoted because it is so straightforward and easy to understand. Jesus came into this world to save the world. The people of Israel were making a good start, but they too often went astray. God loved the Israelites and wanted them to get back on course. All of the first disciples of Jesus were Israelites, and their mission began with the people of Israel.

It wasn't until Paul began his ministry that the Gospels were taken to the gentiles (non-Jews). Jesus' plan was to begin with his own people and then carry the message out to the world. Two thousand years later, we are still struggling to take the "Good News" of Jesus Christ to the whole world. There are millions of people in the world who have never been exposed to the good news of Jesus Christ. So, we begin to know God by the life of Jesus, which was love for the whole world so that everyone had the opportunity to accept or deny it. May the whole world be saved.

What does it tell us about God and humans? **The relationship is built on love and freedom to choose, called free will, and is**

one of the basic principles of that relationship based on love.
This was not seeking condemnation; it was about salvation. It is
obvious in the Gospels that even His disciples did not get what He
was teaching them some of the time. In the Gospels, Jesus tells
his disciples exactly what He is going to do and how He is going
to do it, and they don't understand it, even when it happens. They
did not want to lose Him, and that is understandable. They
couldn't comprehend that Jesus would always be with them in the
Spirit.

This is another characteristic of Jesus. He is immensely patient
and kind to his followers. There are moments in his ministry where
he must have been very frustrated, but He never gave up trying.
He is still actively patient and reaching out to us. Jesus never gives
up on anyone. We humans are quick to dismiss someone who has
a different point of view. Jesus, who knows us better than we know
ourselves, still loves us and calls us. Jesus will never abandon
anyone.

There are so many people who hate Jesus and hate Christianity.
They all have their reasons based on their personal experience,
culture, and circumstances. There are also billions of people who
love Jesus and have experienced his love for us. This conflict is
called 'spiritual warfare'. It is ongoing, and no one knows when it
will end, but the Bible is confident that the end will be when the
Spirit of Christ rules in every heart. Living the Christian life exposes

one to this battle. There are people who will despise you for being a Christian. They have an opposing spirit in them.

> **The love and patience of God and Jesus Christ is incomprehensible, but that is the revelation of God, we have been given.**

The goal is Heaven on Earth, although we cannot predict when. The important thing to remember is each of us has a role in bringing this about for the sake of our children and their children. If you are sick and tired of a world of constant wars, abject poverty, oppressive systems, and injustice, what are you doing about it? The love and patience of Jesus is the only way of making this a better world. This is God's plan and there is no other plan comparable. This is God's plan!

Jesus took me into the future, where there was Heaven on earth. We visited people living in complete harmony and supporting one another. The whole village took raising children as the most important work to do. People had been given supernatural gifts and there was no want. Worship was a daily activity of the whole community. We could have this world if we chose it instead of the way we live now.

The Person of Jesus

The love and compassion of Jesus was limitless, as we see in so many examples of his teaching, healings, and self-sacrifice. The next chapter is devoted to his miracles, so we will be discussing his words that we have been given. The best collection of Jesus' teachings is in Matthew 5-7, known as the 'Sermon on the Mount'.

There are some teachings that use hyperbole, which is exaggeration, to emphasize a point. This was a very common technique in Jesus' time. For example, Christians have never plucked out their eyes or cut off their hands that offended themselves. These teachings must be understood as making a point in an extremely dramatic way. Most of the Sermon on the Mount is very challenging and sets a very high standard of morality. Jesus' teaching makes us examine our hearts and behavior. The morality that Jesus gives us is the way of love.

Jesus is calling us to follow his example, and that is the goal of life. No one is going to achieve perfection in this lifetime, but they will achieve that complete holiness in Heaven. There are many levels of Heaven, and one will enter the appropriate level of Heaven to grow in sanctification. Every person is unique, and God, who knows us better than we know ourselves, will bring us to the level of Heaven that is best for our continued sanctification. Some are more purified than others and God loves us and will put us where we belong so that we may grow in sanctification. There are countless levels of Heaven, and just the perfect one for you and me.

God does not punish; He rehabilitates his children with patience and love. God will ensure that everyone going to Heaven will get precisely what they need. He loves those who do not go to Heaven, and He has plans for them also. How He will love them is also a mystery.

In this world, we are constantly caught between our animal nature and our spiritual nature. Paul described this contrast in Galatians 5:16-26. Here are a few characteristics of the animal nature in us:

"Fornication, idolatry, sorcery, enmities, strife, jealousy, anger, quarrels, dissensions, factions, envy, drunkenness, carousing, and things like these."

Galatians 5:19-21 [NRSVA]

This is only a brief selection of activities that are barriers to the kingdom of God. The following list from Galatians describe the fruits of the spirit.

"The fruit of the Spirit is love, joy, peace, patience, kindness, generosity, faithfulness, gentleness, and self-control."

Galatians 5:22-23 [NRSVA]

We are brought into this world to learn to choose which path we take, and these lessons are learned every moment of our lives. We will 'reap what we sow'. Too many people do not believe this, even though their experiences prove it to be absolutely true. It is delusional to believe there are no consequences to our actions.

Part of the Good News is that Jesus will forgive our sins if we sincerely confess, repent, and ask for forgiveness. Jesus taught this, and He lived it on the cross. This is one of the hardest teachings of Jesus that people can accept. Your sins can be forgiven if you take them to Him. We pray this in the Lord's prayer, and hopefully, we mean it. What an incredible offer we have before us. Can you believe God loves you so much that your sins can be forgiven? This is one of the striking teachings of the Gospel. This is part of the good news of Jesus Christ. Ask the Holy Spirit if your sins are forgiven.

In my near-death experience, Jesus and the angels gave me a life review, from birth to the present. As I grew into my teen years, it got increasingly painful to watch because I did many really bad things. Jesus shared his sorrow with me as we went through my life. Most importantly, he also shared his incomparable love for me and the hope I would learn to do better. I knew I was forgiven and would try to change my ways.

Jesus was asked, "What must I do to inherit eternal life?" He answered, "What is written in the Law?" The man replied, "You shall love the Lord your God with all your heart, and with all your soul, and with all your strength, and with all your mind; and your neighbor as yourself." Jesus approved this response *(Luke 10:25-27 [NRSVA])*. This conversation continued with a parable about loving your neighbor, including people one despises. Jesus forgave the men who crucified Him on the cross. The kingdom of Heaven and Heaven on Earth have the exact same standards, and this is the teaching of Jesus.

> *Forgiveness is central to our sanctification.*

Whether you liked school or not and whether you were a good student or not is immaterial to what your life is really about.

> *We are all here to learn from God and, specifically, to learn from Jesus Christ.*

The Person of Jesus

There are many promises, and we will discuss them in another chapter as we investigate Jesus's person. We have more to consider and grow from.

What did Jesus struggle with when he walked the earth? He was conceived of God's spirit as a fetus in Mary's womb and then was born into the world as a baby. Over time, He matured fully human and in awareness. That means Jesus experienced the human condition and went through the process of human development. He was completely ignorant of his divinity. The scripture tells us He emptied Himself of divinity and took on human form. As He matured, He became aware of his divinity. Jesus grew in wisdom just as we do, because He was fully human, but went far beyond us.

Jesus' life was not a pretense of being human. Over time and with maturity, He discovered His divinity, and this process of development can be discerned in the Gospels. We know little about His early life, but what we know is illuminating. Jesus' father, Joseph, died sometime before Jesus was thirty. In that world, Jesus would have been responsible for the survival of His mother, Mary, and His siblings.

They lived in the very poor village of Nazareth (population of 200-500 people). The only available work was in Sepporis, which was a growing city and a forty-five-minute walk from Nazareth. Since Joseph is identified as a carpenter, it is probable that Jesus had learned that trade from his father and that they had both worked in Sepporis together. Although it is unlikely he had a shop anywhere; he was likely a typical craftsman or construction worker among hundreds. This is a less romantic picture of Jesus' early life. The good news is that in Sepporis, Jesus was exposed to Greek and Roman culture, which explains why Jesus used Greek words in his ministry at times. He was also familiar with Roman culture and made references to it. The question of what He was learning about His divinity is impossible to know because of lack of information. All we know is at the beginning of His ministry, He knew He was connected to God in a powerful way. In Nazareth, He attended synagogue and learned His Jewish faith.

We can speculate on His process of self-realization, and that helps us appreciate His development and our development in this life. The psychoanalytic definition of ego is 'the self-assertive and self-preserving tendency.' (Webster's Dictionary). In simple language, we are wired to survive and thrive. In many respects, this is who we are. There have been exceptions of people that are unusually empathetic and who sacrifice themselves for others.

Jesus certainly did see himself as the Messiah, which was a widely known hope of the Israelites for hundreds of years. There were many false messiahs in Israel who appeared. This leads us to the obvious question of whether he was the true Messiah or just another delusional character who thought he was the Messiah.

There is a direct way to answer that question.

"You shall know them by their fruits."

Matthew 7:16 [NRSVA]

What did Jesus accomplish in his brief three years of ministry? What was Jesus' impact on the people who knew him? What has been the result of his ministry over two thousand years? How has Jesus transformed the lives of millions of people in the past and today? Science relies on the basic concept of evidence-based decision-making. The answers to the previous questions produce sufficient evidence that Jesus was who he said he was. Any rational assessment of Jesus would come to this conclusion. The fact, supported by the evidence, is that Jesus was far more than just a human being. If you don't call that God, then what do you call it?

There are many people who consider Jesus an enlightened master like so many others. When one compares Jesus to other avatars, the comparisons fail the test of common attributes.

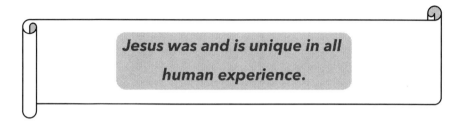

Jesus was and is unique in all human experience.

We have given Him titles like 'Messiah', 'King of Kings', 'Savior', 'Son of God', 'Lamb of God' and more, but these are inadequate in describing Him. He is also known widely as 'friend', and this is meant in a powerful and intimate way. **The people that really know Him call Him 'the only reality'.** This may seem an over-the-top description, but if you succeed in having an intimate relationship with Jesus, you will know Him as your reality. Through the abiding presence of the Holy Spirit, He is always with us.

The Promises of Jesus

4

The Promises of Jesus

"For my eyes have seen your salvation, which you have prepared in the presence of all peoples, a light for the revelation to the gentiles and for the glory to your people Israel."

Luke 2:30-23 [NRSVA]

There are many promises that Jesus made. We are only considering a sampling of them in this chapter arranged by themes. To get a more thorough knowledge of the promises of Jesus, one must read the Gospels. There are more than one hundred promises, and they need to be read in the context in which they were given.

The first selection covers promises concerning discipleship. What are the expectations of a follower of Jesus and what are the consequences?

Following Jesus

Matthew 5:3-11 is known as the Sermon on the Mount and is very all-encompassing about what Jesus promises for those who have put their trust in Him. It has often been said that these statements turn worldly wisdom upside-down. This is an accurate description of them. In nine statements, Jesus states blessedness (exceeding happiness) for awful events that happen in life.

Many books have been written on the meaning of the Sermon on the Mount and they are well worth reading to give insight into the meaning of such challenging statements. This may sound like reward for good behavior, but this is an injustice to what Jesus is saying. These blessings are the faith response to suffering and injustice when a person of real, abiding faith in Jesus suffers, grieves, and is persecuted with all the pain that any human would experience. The difference is that a disciple of Jesus is not consumed by that pain. In the story of the first martyr, Stephen, he is filled with bliss while he is being stoned to death. **The history of Christianity is filled with individuals being gruesomely tortured to death and they respond with praises to God and the singing of spiritual songs.** These testimonials are also unbelievable, and they even get more bizarre when oftentimes these Christian responses to torment lead to the conversion of the tormenters. This is precisely what happened to the Roman soldier who crucified Jesus. *(Luke 23:47).*

Anyone who has had the experience of Heaven would want to be there forever and not in this world. Heaven is joy, love, and peace beyond description. There is none of the pain, suffering, disappointments, chaos, and evils of this world in Heaven. Heaven is the reward for the trials and tribulations we have endured here. May we meet in Heaven someday.

In John 14:12-14, Jesus tells his disciples that they will do what He has been doing, and He tells them if they ask for anything in His name then He will do it. Keep in mind that since Jesus is God, He is omniscient, and He knows what is best. That definitely means He gives us the best gifts and not necessarily what we think we want. Understand that you may ask Jesus for the winning lottery numbers, but it is extremely unlikely you will get them. You can ask for a Mercedes Benz, but do you think that is what God has in mind for you? Here is a tough idea to accept: When a dying person asks for a miracle healing and instead, they die, is that God's good gift? Do you consider going to eternal bliss in Heaven something better than this world? Everyone is going to die, so the questions are when, how, and why. We don't know any of the answers, but God knows and faith grounds us in the fundamental truth that God is omniscient, omnipotent, and good. Read Luke 11:11-13 for the answer.

Charity

"When you give to the needy, do not let your left hand know what your right hand is doing, so that your giving may be in secret."

Matthew 6:3-4 [NRSVA]

This is pretty straightforward and must be taken seriously. Bragging and making a show of charitable acts is out. Charitable works are to be done in humility and discreetly. This act of love is between you and God and no one else.

Anger, revenge, hurt, and unforgiveness are acids in our souls. They will erode us from the inside. Charity is acts of kindness and love. Charity is healing and cleansing. If you do charitable work, you will find joy and purpose.

Forgiveness

Matthew 6:14 states in so many words that as you forgive, you will be forgiven. Jesus speaks about forgiveness frequently and teaches us to pray that in the Lord's Prayer. Forgiveness is the art of letting go of anger, hate, vengeance, and retribution. It is a healing of the person who forgives and may or may not have any response from the offender. When we hold on to these negative emotions, no matter how much we feel justified in those feelings, we are putting a barrier between ourselves and God. Forgiveness frees us from this separation from God which is the very definition of sin. Of course, everyone feels anger when they are offended or hurt. The question is, what do you do with those negative feelings? Jesus tells us to let them go through forgiveness. This is our path to sanctification, which is what the purpose of life is about.

Forgiveness is essential to healing. Every human has been scarred by trauma. Some traumas we have repressed and don't remember. These must be taken to Jesus and ask him to help you forgive. Forgiving is a gift from God that God wants you to have.

Bearing Fruit

John 15:16 states "I chose you and appointed you to go and bear fruit – fruit that will last." If you have any question about your faith in God, then look carefully at the fruits of your efforts. Presumably the work that you are doing was the result of a call from Jesus. If it has been productive, then you can be assured it was a true calling. If you have been unproductive, you have been mistaken or have deceived yourself. Of course, there are hardships, obstacles, and failures, as there is with everything we undertake, but what are the results? Jesus will equip those he calls to success ultimately. To illustrate the difficulty of discerning a call, consider the following. The majority of persons who enter seminary training to become pastors do not become pastors. The majority of pastors serve churches for only a few years before they leave ministry for good. The only comprehensive explanation is they were not called to this vocation by Jesus. They discover this by trial and error.

"You shall know them by their fruits" is not just applicable to Christians (Matthew 7:16). It is also very useful in discerning all humans beyond appearances. Con artists are charming and appeal to anything they determine will win one's favor. Too many politicians are highly successful frauds. This is also true for some pastors.

Discernment is one of the most important lessons we are to learn in this world. Look at the fruits of the person and make an evidence-based decision about whether they are what they pretend to be.

After two years of attending church, I felt strongly that I was being called by God to go into ministry. My wife was strongly opposed. I talked to many pastors and Christian friends, and they encouraged me. When I began seminary, it was one of the happiest times of my life. I excelled in my classes and was sorry that after those three-and-a-half years, my formal studies were over. I loved being a pastor and knew my call was the right decision. I served for thirty years.

Good Gifts

"If you then, though you are evil, know how to give good gifts to your children, how much more will your Father in Heaven give the Holy Spirit to those who ask him!"

Luke 11:11-13 [NIV]

The good gifts come from the Holy Spirit, which is the indwelling Spirit of Christ. What are the gifts of the Spirit?

"The fruit of the Spirit is love, joy, peace, patience, kindness, generosity, faithfulness, gentleness, [and] self-control."

Galatians 5:22-23 [NAB]

These are what Jesus is referring to and not worldly things. Our culture is obsessed with defining success by wealth and big numbers. In our culture, one is judged a failure if one is poor and/or one does not produce big numbers compared to others. The quality of results is more problematic and frequently ignored. How many students pass the test or graduate is what is valued rather than the quality of education and the character of the student. **A student may have passed the tests and been certified qualified for a job, but the employer discovers they are lazy or dishonest and fires them.**

Too often a person hires an attorney because of a legal situation and sadly discovers their lawyer is only interested in making money and not interested in justice. Or we hire a plumber, and the job is poorly done. This is why we desperately require the Holy Spirit to discern who to trust and what fruits this individual produces.

Joy

> *"I have told you this so that my joy may be in you and that your joy may be complete."*
>
> *John 15:11 [NIV]*

What is not to love about this promise of Jesus? Have you ever heard the saying 'Christians are baptized in vinegar'? A follower of Jesus would be full of joy and that is not hard to discern.

Joy is the same emotion as bliss, and to be filled with joy means you are richly blessed. To know you are very blessed means you are being sanctified.

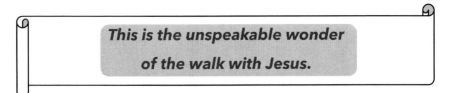

This is the unspeakable wonder of the walk with Jesus.

This is why a follower of Jesus has to sing those worship songs, pray those prayers in a group of like-minded people, listen to the words of the Bible accompanied by commentary from the preacher, and participate in rituals based on traditions. **This is called church because it is a safe place to express and share the joy of being in an intimate relationship with Jesus, the Son of God.**

Teaching

"Go therefore and make disciples of all nations, baptizing them in the name of the Father and of the Son and of the Holy Spirit and teaching them to obey everything I have commanded you. And remember, I am with you always, to the end of the age."

Matthew 28:19-20 [NRSVA]

This promise and command of Jesus is one of the most significant and ignored verses in the Gospels. For most of the two thousand years of Christianity, only a select few very devout people followed this scripture. These were typically the trained and supported missionaries, evangelists, and teachers selected by the Church to do this work. The vast majority of Christians were excused and excluded from these tasks and were expected to offer financial support for the few who went into the world. **Going out into the world spreading the faith was for professionals and not for the 'unwashed masses'.**

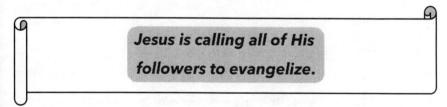

Jesus is calling all of His followers to evangelize.

This was just another example of the church controlling as much as they could.

Some are called to spread the Gospel to their family and that is their calling. Some are called to spread the Gospel in their community. Some are called to go overseas to foreign nations. Each individual is responsible for their own calling, and this is far more than a feeling. Some of the considerations about the sense of being called must be tested in these ways: is the call supported by the reality of the individual's situation such as family responsibilities, educational background and necessary skills, the assessment of dangers and success, and how do mature Christians react to what is described as one's call. If wise Christians support the idea, then one has a green light. If wise Christians oppose one's sense of call, that is a red light. We humans are masters of self-deception, and it is imperative that we rely on persons wiser and more mature in their faith journey than ourselves.

Burdens

Matthew 11:29-30 is essential guidance to equip a follower of Jesus in this journey. This scripture refers to being yoked to Jesus and sharing the burdens. This is so important because **following Jesus can be overwhelmingly discouraging in many disparate ways. We all indulge ourselves in occasional delusions of grandeur.** The vast majority of time we are humbled in our efforts to spread the Good News of Jesus Christ. Ask anyone who has been passionately doing this for a lifetime. They will tell you they have been humbled by circumstances and that amazing results have also happened.

When one looks objectively at successes you will find it was God who was behind the success and your efforts were only a small contribution. To illustrate this, we look at 'saving souls'.

The first point is that only God saves souls. Human beings do not save souls, not even their own. Secondly, we have an important contribution to participation in saving souls. We can till the ground, water the seedling, and weed the soil, but only God creates the seed and gives the growth. We must yoke ourselves to Jesus and let him share in the burdens. If we try to go it alone, we are doomed to fail. If we carry the burdens we are being oppressed by, we will fail. Give Jesus the part of the load that has you stuck in the muck. Let go of the pridefulness and ask for help. Jesus is passionate about caring about us and lifting the load off of us. Jesus never gives us more than we can carry. We give our burdens to Jesus. We let God be our strength.

Being human, I struggle with all the vices of pridefulness, guilt, self-doubt, and more. In prayer with the Spirit of Christ, I see my faults and I see my way to follow Jesus as he would have me do things. In a clergy group that I belonged to, there was a pastor who always mocked me and hurt my feelings. I hated him. I took this to Jesus, and He told me to love him and not to respond to the nasty things that he said. In a few months, we became friends, and the problem went away. Take all your burdens to Jesus and listen.

Kindness

Matthew 25:31-46 is the most specific and clear set of instructions on following Jesus in all the Gospels. Some of Jesus' sayings are open to interpretation and **some can be misunderstood due to being taken out of context or lack of knowledge of the original Hebrew or Greek.** The words of Jesus in Matthew 25 are perfectly clear. Christians perform acts of kindness, also known as charity. The word charity comes from the Latin 'charitas' meaning 'acts of love'.

Conversely, false Christians do not engage in these acts of kindness/love. They make a show of being followers, but they do not show up in the trenches doing the work. Jesus gives examples such as feeding the hungry, giving drink to the thirsty, inviting the stranger into your life, clothing those who need clothes, caring for the sick, and visiting those in prison. These are the examples Jesus used for acts of love. The list of acts of love is inexhaustible and anyone can add numerous examples of these kindnesses that they have received and have given.

In the mission work that I have done, the funds have always come without me fundraising. The money just comes in the tens of thousands. The church that I found after my near-death experience, the mission work I have been blessed to do, my understanding of theology, and the support of mature Christians are some examples of Jesus' gifts to me. He is exceedingly generous when we do our best to follow him.

Eternal Life

John 14 contains a vivid and comprehensive description of what happens to followers of Jesus in the promise of Heaven. We will consider just a fraction of what is contained in Chapter 14 of John's Gospel. In John 14:3, Jesus promises that "I will come again and will take you to myself, so that where I am, there you may be also." [NRSVA]. Do you know that when you die, if you have put your faith in Jesus, he will come to you and take you home to Heaven? In searching world religions, there are no other promises like these. This is very personal and comforting.

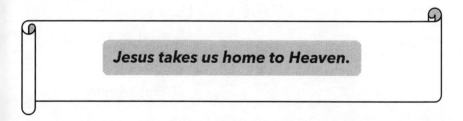

Jesus takes us home to Heaven.

When I called out to Jesus in my wretched state in Hell, He came to me. He reached down and touched me with His hands and I became whole. I was totally filled with His great love and all the pain had vanished. He gently picked me up and embraced me against Himself. He stroked my back, like a parent with a child. I knew I was safe, loved, and accepted just as I was. This has been the high point of my life.

In John 14:6-7, Jesus says "I am the way, the truth, and the life. No one comes to the Father except through me. If you know me, you will know my Father also." [NRSVA]. Both here and throughout John 14, Jesus unequivocally states that He and God are one. Jesus is presenting us with the obvious, that following Him is following God. One could also reverse this and say that following God by Jesus' example is following Jesus. This statement speaks volumes about the inclusiveness of God's love and is not about exclusive love. Those who love "the way, the truth, and the life" are coming to God in Heaven and they are being escorted by Christ Jesus. This is the most wonderful and encouraging promise of God.

What Does Jesus Expect?

5

What Does Jesus Expect?

"Truly I tell you, whoever does not receive the Kingdom of God as a little child will never enter it."

Mark 10:15 [NRSVA]

What does any parent expect of their children? The answer is a lot. Jesus also expects a lot from us; He wants everything. This may sound frightening but is in fact not.

First, Jesus wants passionately for us to receive His love. God through Christ created us. We are God's children, His creation. He loves us and only wants the best for us, like any good parent.

Having a relationship with Jesus is experiencing His love, which is overwhelming and beyond anything we have known in this world. When I earnestly seek His love, I am completely filled with it. This is not some casual thing; rather, Jesus' love is beyond words, and when you receive it, you will know that it is the most awesome thing in your life. I have to feel that love periodically to keep me going in this life. Find that great love for yourself.

Words are inadequate to describe the love of God because until you have experienced this great love, you have no true understanding or knowledge of what God's love is.

> *We have known many forms of love in our lives, but they do not really compare with the magnitude of God's love. How can you describe an ocean by examining a cup of water?*

There may be a few similarities, but they are hopelessly inadequate. Since the word love has never been well defined in all human literature, the following will be a futile attempt to describe some of the characteristics of God's love which a person will know in an intimate relationship with Jesus. God's great love is transformative.

The irony is that we are using words to explain something which is beyond words and beyond the ordinary experiences of life in this world. There is no useful vocabulary for spiritual facts. There is a Gospel song that says, 'I know that I know that I know'. For those that have encountered the love of Jesus, this is a profound truth and cannot be explained. In Zen Buddhism, there is a famous saying: 'he who knows does not say, and he who says does not know'. There are some things beyond words, like love.

The mystery of God's love cannot be described, but it can be experienced, and it is by millions of people if they are willing to receive it. This willingness requires letting go of every expectation and preconception. Simply put, it is openness of the heart, mind, and soul. Another way of describing this is unconditional love, which is called in Greek agape. Most of the love we know is conditional, better known as 'strings attached'. God's love has no strings attached, so when one responds to this Agape love, one doesn't have to do anything but bask in that love and receive it.

When a person receives love, particularly agape love, one wants to respond in some way. How can one respond to a love so great that it can never be repaid and never was 'deserved'. What did we do to earn this love? The obvious answer is, we did nothing, and we also did things opposed to this love.

The Bible tells us we are all sinners, but God wants us in Heaven forever, commonly called salvation. The answer is because God made us, we are God's children, and God loves us, flaws and all. God has gone to extreme measures to reach us with unconditional love. This is the main theme of the whole Bible. The story is told by illustrations of triumphs and failures of humans to receive and love God in return, both in the Hebrew Testament and in the New Testament. God is always merciful and reaching out to those who know the true God.

> **Love is a reciprocal relationship and that means that love demands acceptance or rejection.**

Consider how many times and in how many ways you have neglected, rejected, or dismissed the approach of God in your life. When you critically examine your part, you will find that the door has been opened to you and you walked away. A sweet, kindly grandparent who tried to talk to you about Jesus or a song you heard that deeply touched your heart and then you quickly moved on to another distraction. We struggle with too many delusions of 'important things to do'. The fact is that the most important thing to do in life is to have an intimate relationship with God. This is what life is all about, to love God with all your heart, mind, soul, and strength and to love your neighbor as yourself (Mark 12:30-31). How hard is this to understand?

If you have experienced God's love, you feel compelled to do something with that overflowing, wonderful love. This is not required; it is a deep compulsion to do something. Let's look at a few responses to this great agape love.

What about loving our neighbor as we love ourselves? This simple commandment begins by kindness, gentleness, compassion, patience, generosity, forgiveness, and community. These are all the prerequisites for loving our neighbor. We all need more of these qualities. We seem to never have enough of these qualities, but we can cultivate them, and when we do, we discover we have having fruitful lives loving others as we have been loved.

Before we go any further, it is necessary to define the word sin. **The standard definition is alienation from God or intentional separation from God.** It is important to emphasize the intentional significance of sin. Every moment of our lives we make choices. Because we are conscious beings, these choices are made quickly and usually without much thought. And there are situations when we have to make a choice immediately, such as in an emergency. Sometimes, our choice is to fight or flee. Fight or flight may not be the right response, and taking a moment to think rationally could be the best response to a frightening situation.

You're driving down the highway thinking about what you are going to do at your destination, and someone cuts you off and then unexpectedly slows down. What are you going to do? Smash into their car and teach them a lesson, or hit your brakes to prevent a collision and then try and pass them and get as far away as possible? This is fight or flee. These occasions happen without warning, and how we react is critical to our well-being.

How do you react when a neighbor insults you? Do you give it back to them with an insult or do you walk away? Do you say, "I'm sorry I hurt you. I didn't mean that," or "Sorry you feel that way?" Can you let it go? Do you understand it really is not about you, it is all about them? Why they are offensive, you will probably never know. Maybe someday they will apologize but you don't know the future. Maybe someday they will confide in you why they were angry that day, but who knows what will happen to them. The point of all of this is we have a choice, and that choice has consequences. Loving your neighbor is comparable to loving God. Your neighbor can be a complete stranger who is repulsive to you. Your neighbor can be someone you have never seen before, like a child who is lost and afraid. Caring for that little one is loving God. Walking away from confrontation is loving God. Avoiding violence is loving God.

During my prison ministry, I met several very fine people who had made terrible choices in their lives. They admitted and regretted what they had done. They needed rehabilitation, not hopeless confinement, which was all they got. There is good in almost all people.

This world is vastly complex and beyond comprehension. Our job is the immediate world around us. Family, friends, co-workers, strangers, and the unknown are our world that we are responsible for. Our anger, desire to control, preconceived opinions, needs, and self-centred desires are the issues that we need to deal with. Are we capable of enough insight to be better than our base instincts? Yes, if we do the work of self-analysis and spend the time and energy to look deep into our feelings and the reasons why we have those feelings. Praying to God for help in these struggles can be very rewarding.

My life review vividly showed me the effect of my interactions with other people and what they felt and thought. This was very revealing, and it was often horrifying to know that my self-centered ways of manipulating others drove them away from me. Like everyone, I wanted to be loved, respected, and wise, but I was often producing the opposite results. Since my life review, I have tried to be kinder, more sympathetic, and guided by the Spirit of Christ.

What are our reasons? What is our history that causes us to feel and react this way? What traumas have programmed us emotionally? This is tough stuff to deal with, but it is the work we need to do. We can also choose to change who we are and how we react. With the help of God, nothing is impossible, including changing ourselves.

Is it true that we really want to be loved? Do we know a God who is love? Is it possible to be a loving person whose life is pleasing to God? Hopefully, you agree with the previous statements. This is what God wants. God also knows we make mistakes, and God forgives us our mistakes when we bring those sins to God and ask for forgiveness. Jesus guaranteed our forgiveness on the cross, and we are forgiven when we bring it to Him. We can be free of our sins and pure before God if we believe and give it all to Jesus. How about getting rid of all those spots and stains all over your soul and having no more anxiety about your worth to God. Living a life knowing that you and God are in a good relationship and that God has your back is a wonderful way to live in this world. May our loving God be your foundation.

The love of Jesus Christ is a constant in my life. Sometimes it is very present, and other times, I desperately seek it because I need to feel it. Jesus told me that He is always with me. I know this is true, but when I am not feeling His presence, it is because I am distracted by many things, and not because He has abandoned me. It is my responsibility to restore the relationship.

Does Jesus Know You?

6

Does Jesus Know You?

"When Jesus saw Nathaniel coming toward him, he said of him 'Here is truly an Israelite in whom there is no deceit'."

John 1:47 [NRSVA]

One of the greatest mysteries in the world is the incarnation of God in the person of Jesus Christ two thousand years ago. This mysterious event was witnessed by hundreds of people and radically changed human history. Billions of people have believed this to be true and many of them have had miraculous experiences of the power of this truth. There are also doubters who dismiss this as nonsense. One has the choice to accept the truth of Jesus as the incarnation of God or to dismiss it. Hopefully, you will put it to the test and decide for yourself what is true and what is false.

> *The power of God's love is enough to convince anyone of the truth about Jesus being fully man and fully God, which is the great mystery.*

One of the wonderful things about the incarnation is that Jesus really gets us. When we do something good, we can feel Jesus' approval. This goes for little things as well as big things. Controlling our temper when someone puts us down is pleasing Jesus. Making a charitable contribution with no expectation of reward pleases Jesus. Not blaming God when we have a disappointment pleases Jesus. Kindness, which is so simple, pleases Jesus.

If you want to know Jesus, we have four testimonies that describe him in the Bible, and they are called the Gospels. It is critically important that one reads them and studies them. If one is serious about knowing God, this is the only way to really know God through the person of Jesus. It is a unique gift that God has given us to have this intimacy with a God who is unknowable and has revealed this much of God's character. Of course, there is much more to God than what is revealed in the person of Jesus, but there is more in the Gospels than any person can possibly comprehend. Jesus is Christ and is the perfect revelation of God for us humans. God is so vast and great that we cannot possibly handle that much knowledge of the whole of God, but God, in His great love for his children, has revealed to us as much as we can handle through Jesus Christ. Studying the Gospels is a lifetime of receiving new revelations when one lets the Holy Spirit guide you to the truth. This resource has no end when you give yourself over to the Holy Spirit's guidance.

Jesus sent us the Holy Spirit so that we may know the truth. The Holy Spirit literally speaks to us and guides us when we are open to the Spirit. I warn you, there are counterfeit spirits, but only one Holy Spirit. If the spirit is one hundred percent consistent with the Gospels, then that is the Holy Spirit. If the Spirit contradicts the Gospels in any way, that is a counterfeit spirit and must be expelled from your life. The evil one is the master of deception. So many are led astray by false spirits. They masquerade as God, angels, Jesus, and saints, but they are taking you down the wrong path. The Holy Spirit is known as the Spirit of Truth, the Spirit of God, the Spirit of Jesus, and the Spirit. This is our only way. This Spirit is our truth. This Spirit is our life. It looks like Jesus, talks like Jesus, and acts like Jesus. If you want to please God and live a life that leads you to Heaven, you have your guide.

When we get to Heaven, we will greatly expand our knowledge, love, and enjoyment of our intimacy with God. That journey begins with our indwelling relationship with the Spirit of Christ when we ask that Spirit into our hearts, minds, and souls. This is the beginning of salvation, which is a life-long endeavor.

People say that God has never spoken to them. People who have genuinely asked Jesus to be their savior are given the Holy Spirit, and that is God talking to them. This whole book is being guided by the Holy Spirit. One can be open to the Spirit and live by that guidance. It may sound crazy, but you can have God speaking to you all the time through the indwelling Spirit of Jesus Christ. God speaks to us in our hearts, and one has to listen. What this means is that the Spirit speaks to the core of our being and not to our ears. You may hear the Spirit of Christ speak in a Bible study by a fellow speaker. You may hear the Spirit speak in a song on the radio. You may even hear the Spirit speak anywhere.

When the Spirit tells us something, it is perfectly clear. The Spirit is frequently surprising in its messages, telling one to do something different than what they thought they were going to do.

The Spirit also warns of danger and avoiding trouble. The Spirit will never steer you wrong. You don't have to obey the Spirit, but why would you not trust it?

Imagine there is a person who always belittles you in a group you belong to, and it is driving you nuts. The Spirit tells you to befriend that person and you react by telling the Spirit that advice is wrong because this person does not want to be friends. The Spirit says that this person is insecure and wants your friendship and that you should go out of your way to be friendly. Surprisingly, over a period of time, this works, and that individual ceases to make critical remarks. The Spirit knows what it is doing, and you have gained a friend who used to be an adversary.

Jesus walked the walk. Think about Jesus spending time with His disciples, walking around the Holy Land preaching, healing, and just doing the human experience. He knew exhaustion, discouragement, rejection, confrontation, and being misunderstood. The Gospels are brutally honest about Jesus' ministry. The Gospels show Jesus struggling with the human and the divine, just like we do, despite Him being without sin. We are always struggling with the flesh and the Spirit.

Jesus endured the entire human experience, and he gathered up his strength and faith and went on despite discouragement and rejection.

One of the reasons Jesus was mobbed was because of his ability to heal people. In his world, many people suffered terrible pain from injury, sickness, and disease. There were no cures, doctors were useless, and the people suffered. When the word went out about him, that he healed, people rushed to him from far and near. He healed them by the hundreds everywhere he went. Jesus healed physical and spiritual problems, which were called demonic possession. Today we often call these psychological problems, but are we missing something? Treating people with psychoactive drugs works sometimes, but maybe the cure is something deeper that we are ignoring. The point is, Jesus was involved everywhere he went with very needy people. He served them and ministered to them. One needs to be aware that Jesus is still healing today, both physical problems and demonic oppression. To build our love, hope and faith, we are always tested by the demonic. Being human, we have many weaknesses that can become our strengths. Reading Ephesians 6:10-17 gives us clear guidance about standing firm in our faith by "putting on the whole armor of God." The only power evil has over us is the power that we give it.

One of Jesus' greatest frustrations was how little his disciples were really listening to his teachings. The Gospels provide examples of Jesus telling his disciples very direct things and his disciples contradicting him, telling him he was wrong. Jesus said things that they could not handle.

When we read the Gospels, we read things Jesus said that we find repellant. For example, Jesus says, "Love your enemies." Can you love your enemies? They are enemies because they are rotten, evil people. We despise them because of who they are.

Give me a break, Jesus. I am not going to love them. I don't care what you say; and while we are on the topic, why did you seek crucifixion when you could have had a long ministry instead of three short years? Why submit to crucifixion?

We can argue with Jesus, just like his disciples did. Jesus is a tough Savior to understand and follow because His standards are so high that we sometimes get discouraged about ever being good enough. Jesus is a tough Savior because when we rely on His strength, He is always victorious. When we rely on our strength, we are vulnerable. Thanks be to God that we have a tough Savior. No one, including the saints, has ever gotten it perfectly right. Read the lives of the saints and learn of their struggles to be fully obedient to the teachings of Jesus.

Don't despair, because Jesus knows us, and He gets us. He just wants us to do our best, and that is good enough. Jesus loved His disciples despite their shortcomings, which were plentiful. Jesus loves you just the way you are. Do you think Jesus loves His handiwork? Yes, Jesus loves His creatures and just wants the best for them. It breaks His heart when they are cruel and violent. It delights Him when his creatures are kind and loving. Choose what you want to do with your life. You can live life freely in this world being self-centered, cruel, greedy, exploiting others, and creating mayhem everywhere you go; or you can be as kind, loving, and generous as you are able. One way is sticking a knife into the heart of Jesus and the other is receiving and responding to his love. Make your choice.

In the life after this one, you will receive your reward. During my near-death experience, I learned from Jesus that our reward for doing our sincere best in following his teaching is the overwhelming wonderful life in Heaven forever and ever. God made us free to choose. The life after this one is eternal and may be wonderful beyond words in Heaven, or it may be torment beyond words in Hell. Which will you choose by the life you live?

How About Miracles

7

How About Miracles

"And he did the same with the cup after supper, saying, this cup that is poured out for you is the new covenant in my blood."

Luke 22:20 [NRSVA]

Look around, and you will see miracles everywhere, but I suggest you start with a mirror. Do you appreciate what you are? You are a colony of seventy-five trillion cells that all work harmoniously to keep you functioning. Every day, millions of cells die, and millions of new cells replace the old ones. You were born from a single cell that was fertilized by your father, and this cell multiplied and grew in your mother's womb for nine months and out you came into the world. As you grew, your brain began to absorb information and you learned how to function in the world. Something amazing happened during this process which is unique in the whole animal kingdom. You developed self-consciousness. All animals think, but you can think about your thinking. Simply put, you have awareness. You know what you know. You can ask a question and answer a question. Unlike a monkey, dog, or lion, you can comprehend complex information and retain it for future reference. Human existence is a miracle. One should appreciate the opportunity you have to exist in such a state of being. Even a handicapped person can have this gratitude to be alive and aware.

Let's consider one more miracle before we go to specifics, and that is our home. Our home is planet earth, and it is a miracle beyond comprehension. In our solar system, it is the only habitable planet. The Earth was born four and a half billion years ago and evolved into the world it is today, although some Christians believe it is only six thousand years old - either way, it is an incalculable amount of time. Where did the water come from that fills the oceans? No one knows the answer. When the earth was forming, there was no water because the earth was red hot molten rock. Where did the atmosphere come from? Scientists speculate about its origin and evolution. How is it we have a stable orbit around the sun that keeps the temperature of our planet pleasantly moderate. The miracles of our planet go on and on, and then we go into the miracle of life. What role did God play in creating our world and life? We can speculate but we cannot give definite answers because there is no proof. Our world is a miracle, and it gives us a beautiful home. God has patiently directed and planned the evolution of our planet. This is God's creation and was no accident. God put everything together over millions of years so that we would have a beautiful beginning on Earth.

Jesus told me, "There is no contradiction between scientific truth and Biblical truth. They are two different ways of viewing the wonders of who God is and who we are." When we seek God's love and God's truth in our lives, we become one with God, which is sanctification. There is no time limit in Heaven, and complete sanctification will happen when we are ready, willing, and able.

There are miracles that we all get to witness, such as the birth of a baby. Have you ever had the opportunity to be at a birth or even give birth? You know that baby is a miracle, and that this brand-new human being has so much potential for life. It is amazing to be present at a birth and even more amazing to be the one who carries that baby in her womb and see it come into this world. What unconditional love a mother feels for her child.

Have you ever watched dragonflies? Have you ever really looked at a tree? Have you ever studied an ant colony? The world is filled with endless wonder; it is made of miracles. This leads us to the meaning of the word miracle.

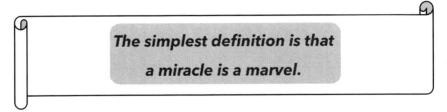

The simplest definition is that a miracle is a marvel.

The longer definitions use words like extraordinary, abnormal, or an event brought about by superhuman agency. So, a miracle can be anything, anywhere, at any time. Striking a match in the dark is not miraculous, however, in a cave where there is absolutely no light and the striking of a match illuminates the whole cave, it can seem so. The fact that a single match can light up a whole cave is awesome. The real miracle is the eye, which is so sensitive to light that it requires only a small number of lumens to see. Did you ever really appreciate your vision? Hopefully, you will never have vision loss, because then you will appreciate what you had, too late.

Please consider your life and the world around as miracle after miracle. Are you looking for healing miracles? Well, they happen every day in hospitals. We must acknowledge the knowledge and skill of the doctors. Just as important is the love and caring of the nurses. There is also a whole team of caregivers who clean, take blood pressure, and deliver food that make healing possible. Do you think that healing is solely the result of procedures doctors prescribe? No, that is only a part.

There is another part in the miracle of healing which is spiritual, and this is often the most important part of healing. It is called faith.

> *A person who has no faith has less chance of healing, and a person with a strong faith has a greater chance of healing.*

Faith can and does produce miracles. If you doubt any of this, go and talk to doctors to examine the truth of the importance of faith in healing.

Faith is powerful and nearly impossible to scientifically investigate. Faith is believing in something bigger or greater than oneself. Faith means trusting in a favorable outcome.

When Jesus walked the earth, he said he could not heal people where there was no faith (Mark 6:4-6). Jesus healed people who were strangers that came to him with one thing in common. Out of desperation, they believed he could heal them, and he did. How did he heal them? Because he was both fully human and fully divine, he made them well. He did these healings out of compassion and asked nothing in return. He healed thousands in his short time on earth and he is still doing this work today.

> *Millions have been healed with the help of Jesus over the past two thousand years.*

What about miracles? If you say you don't believe in miracles, are you blind? Open your eyes and look at nature and all the beauty around you. Just consider your little, tiny self in this vast universe and the tremendous opportunity that you have been given to live and experience this life. Try and put your ego aside for a bit and realize there is more than meets the eye. There is a power and intelligence working behind the scenes that makes all this possible, and we call it God.

Faith and Works

8
Faith and Works

"And the king will answer them, 'Truly I tell you, just as you did it to the least of these who are members of my family, you did it to me.'"

Matthew 25:40 [NRSVA]

There is controversy in some Christian denominations about the importance or even necessity of works versus the paramount importance of faith. There is no question that faith is critical to salvation and there is no substitute. Good works do not substitute for faith. How important are works, then?

How is it possible for a person to have faith in Jesus and to follow him without following his example of works? Jesus was constantly doing good works during his ministry in this world. Anyone who believes in Jesus follows his example.

> *Someone who says they have faith and do not need to do works is a hypocrite or misled.*

If you plant flowers in your yard, do you water them when there has been insufficient rain? Of course. Gardeners water their plants, and that is their works. What if you encounter a person who has planted a garden but didn't water the plants when they were dry? Would they say, "Oh, I believe they will be fine?" So much for faith versus works. No rational person suffers such nonsense.

Let's think about works and what that implies. Probably the most important thing about good works is listening to people before you do anything. It is a huge mistake to think you know what they need and impose that on them. Listen! Listen! Listen! Then involve them in this work you want to do. Get feedback about your progress and intentions before you act.

Of course, the objective of Christian works is to lead people to Jesus Christ, but you need to have a relationship with them before they trust you. Going from place to place evangelizing to strangers is not fruitless, but a lot of that enthusiasm that is expressed after a rousing sermon and alter call can rather quickly be forgotten by disciples over the following days. Becoming interested in and knowing people is the best way to minister to them. To try and change people because we have a big ego and think we know them and their situation better than they do is wrong. You cannot change anyone but yourself. You can only help them when they ask.

Faith and Works

We are going back and forth between faith and works. Ultimately, faith and works become one lifestyle. By faith we are kind and compassionate towards everyone we meet all the time. **Living by faith means looking for and finding the Spirit of Christ in everyone we meet, and everyone includes persons we perceive as our enemies, including criminals, drug addicts, and vagrants.** That is one way we love our enemies. We seek the good in them. Faith is a way of living, and it is not easy. There are people we find repugnant because of their morality or their personal behavior. We don't judge them; we try to love them and bring out the best in them.

During my near-death experience, I learned that I must see both the good and evil in people, which is called discernment. This wisdom to discern the Spirit in people is how we respond appropriately to them. We need to avoid some people because they are toxic to us. We need to befriend some people because they are wiser than we are, and we can learn from them. Discernment is critical to living in this world.

Let me share with you a brief reflection on ministering in the church. I served as a lay minister, student minister, interim minister, and twenty-three years as pastor of seven different churches in my three decades of ministry. It was a decision to go to seminary and become an ordained minister that really equipped me to serve the church of Jesus Christ. The demands of pastoring are endless, and no matter how many hours and days you work, there are always more demands than you can meet.

A few times, people would joke, "Well, you only work one hour a week." I never knew how to respond to that remark. I soon learned that I could only do so much and that I needed the help of members of the church to take on responsibilities to keep the ministries going. One of the constant objects of concern is the state of the property, such as maintenance, problems such as heating, cooling, and breakdowns, improvements to the property, such as roof repairs, window replacements, and walls needing paint, the cost of hiring contractors, and how are we going to pay for these necessary expenses.

There is a saying that "The church is not a business, but it must be run like a business." Keeping the church financially solvent is a very consuming business. Everything you do in a church has a cost, either real or hidden. At every church council meeting, every item becomes a discussion about where to find the money to do these things. The theological reasons were rarely considered because everyone was obsessed with the cost of doing these things.

Faith and Works

One does not turn the Holy Spirit on and off. The Spirit of Christ tells us to love them to the best of our ability. Of course, that does not mean to submit to them or be deceived by them. Hopefully, along with loving them is the spirit of discernment, which guides us into the truth and keeps us from being deceived and staying focused on the Spirit of Christ.

Doing good works must be guided by the Holy Spirit. There is no other way. Ask the Spirit for guidance one your actions. The world is a vast bottomless pit of need, and you can't do anything except your meager little part.

Jesus healed a portion of the people in Israel and the world was filled with millions of people he never met. Your ministry is the people in your face and not the world. It is so easy to be discouraged by how great the needs of the world are, but our job lies with the man, woman, or child in front of us. Love the person you are with, as Jesus did. Loving without discernment is enabling without helping the person.

What if we could enlist more people to help us in the ministry we have chosen? It would be amazing to multiply the work team. You would be surprised at the number of people who are searching for a ministry in which to engage. Presenting what you are doing in a positive light and inviting people to be a part of it will produce results. Maybe you will get one out of fifty or five out of twenty, but there are people eager to do ministry.

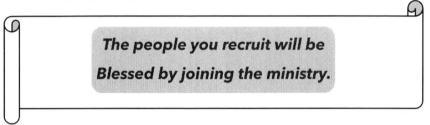

The people you recruit will be Blessed by joining the ministry.

You will also be blessed by giving them the opportunity to serve.

It is very gratifying to invite people to join you, especially young people. Serving in a soup kitchen, going on a mission trip to a different culture, or going on an overseas mission can be life-changing for a young person. The world is telling them to be selfish and get everything for themselves. They are being told their worth is how successful they can be in acquiring wealth and power; they are being seduced by a very materialistic culture. We have the opportunity to show them an alternative to living by sharing the love of Christ Jesus in very meaningful ways. In the developed world, Christianity desperately needs ministries to grow the faith.

In living a life of faith and works, we are going to make mistakes. Remember, there has been only one perfect person, and that is Jesus Christ. You will make many mistakes. Not everything you do will be a miracle, but we persist because we just do our best to keep trying, with the help of God.

Catholic nun Sister Mary Dolores told me after my near-death experience that she and the other sisters prayed for me every day for thirteen years. Because of my near-death experience, their prayers were answered. What would have become of me without the prayers of the Sisters of Notre Dame, I don't know, but I suspect it would not have been good. Thanks be to God that I encountered and was prayed for by those nuns.

One never really knows how God is going to use our puny efforts. Perhaps your time, energy, money, and Christian witness was invested in a person who turned against you and went in the wrong direction. Is it possible that someday they will remember what you said about Jesus and salvation? Is it possible they will remember the kindness and faith you showed to them? Yes, it is possible, and by the grace of God it will happen, although you may never know about it. God is working in the world far beyond what we know. God uses our works in many mysterious ways for good.

The real point of this chapter is to persuade you that faith and works are really one mission. We live our faith and work on our identity. We are trying our best to embody the Spirit of Christ in our thoughts, words, and actions. We do not seek recognition or rewards for what we do. Rather, we seek to please God and let Him do the rest. Just plant and till; God will provide growth. He wants worldwide conversion to the Spirit of Christ. Jesus told me in my near-death experience that God wants everyone to be totally converted to follow God's love, way, truth, and life. This will happen and the world will be totally changed to Heaven on Earth. The Spirit of Christ will rule the world. When this new earth will happen is unknown, but it is coming. Isn't it about time?

The world seems to be a hopeless mess, and maybe the only solution is an apocalypse to bring it all down and for Jesus to come and take control. No one can argue against this hope. For now, we must not be selfish and live in the security of our own salvation. If you have the Spirit of Christ, you are passionate about bringing everyone into a saving relationship with Jesus Christ. All the suffering people endure is so unnecessary because when you really know Jesus, there are solutions. Knowing Jesus makes even the biggest troubles bearable and is the way to a life of joy, peace, love, hope and faith. If you have these gifts, you want everyone to have them. That is Christian love. Life is a constant struggle because our character is being built by these challenges. By relying on Jesus Christ, we can be victorious over any battle. Not everything goes the way we want but it always goes the way God

Faith and Works

wants, whether we understand it or not. We pray "Thy will be done," not our will be done.

Who is Called?

9
Who is Called?

"Jesus…said, 'those who are well have no need of a physician, but those who are sick; I have come to call not the righteous, but sinners'."

Mark 2:17 [NRSVA]

Since we are all sinners, we are all called to serve God. God calls every human being to a Christlike life. God wants every single person to go to Heaven. God does not want anyone to go to Hell. Sadly, many people are not going to Heaven. Only God knows and only God chooses who is going to Hell. People can speculate all they want about who goes to Heaven and who goes to Hell, and all of that speculation is not worth a cup of spit. There are a significant number of people in this world who have been called to follow Jesus and who have done their best to follow the life of discipleship. These people generally believe in their salvation.

There is another group of people in this world who are not Christians but who have lived Christian lives, and they may be candidates for Heaven. They are called anonymous Christians. By their heart and religious teachings, they have lived by the Spirit of Christ but have never heard the Gospel. May they be blessed because they answered their call.

In Mark 12:30-31, Jesus said that eternal life is for one who "loves God with all your heart, mind, soul, and strength" and those who "love your neighbor as yourself." People who do this are guided by the spirit of Christ regardless of their culture, religious upbringing, or their familiarity with Christianity. These are people who follow the Spirit of Christ all over the world and God knows and loves them.

We might add that **there are plenty of people who call themselves Christians who are not going to Heaven because they are hypocrites**. They can brag and proclaim their faith in Jesus, but do not practice what Jesus taught. If you want to read about true and fake followers of Jesus, read Matthew 25. This lays it out clearly and simply.

Everyone is called to follow the Spirit of Christ because the Spirit of Christ is the Spirit of God. How fortunate are children raised in loving homes where they are taken to church and guided by loving teachers in the Christian faith. How blessed they are to be baptized, confirmed, and given the Holy Spirit to guide them. By contrast, how unfortunate are those raised in violent, dysfunctional homes who never go to church and who have to grow up in the worst environment. How God judges people is a mystery, but we know that God is merciful.

The Way, The Truth and The Life | 110

> *It is strange how wonderful people can rise from a terrible environment and the most horrible people can come from the best environment.*

This is more proof in the power of free will and how the world works.

The most fortunate people in the world are not the wealthiest or the most powerful. The most blessed people in the world are those who are called and who respond to their call. The following are a few examples. A group of women feel called to use their sewing skills to serve the poor. One group makes clothing, which is given away, and another group makes shopping bags for the homeless. These women have answered their call. Go to any hospital and you will find hundreds of people who have been called to a healing ministry. They make a living doing what God has called them to do, and that is wonderful. Most pastors make less money than schoolteachers. Some have jobs to support their families while they serve a church, and they are answering their call. There are a tiny few superstar pastors who are wealthy building megachurches that they have been called to create. The list of those called is endless depending on how a person is serving God in their profession. **A carpenter becomes a real craftsman and does beautiful work, and he is answering his call.**

Everyone is called. The question is how they respond to it. One can ignore their call because they think they have something more important to do. The world is full of distractions, and pleasing God is not that important to some. Pleasing God should be top priority, but getting a new car, buying a bigger house, fighting for a promotion at work, etc. can be big distractions. What is more important than being obedient to God? Many people don't see it this way. They are in for an unpleasant surprise when they leave this life and go into the afterlife. **These people go to Hell and that is an existence experiencing the pain one inflicted on others.** My experience of Hell was specifically for me and is not the only way Hell is for other people. I found myself in complete darkness, surrounded by people who hated me and who tore me apart. If I chose words to describe what it was it was like, I would say utter hopelessness. Obedience to God is not optional.

How do you know what you are called to do? There are several ways to discern your calling. First, what does your heart care about? Where is your passion in this world? Look into ways you can satisfy your deepest interest in pleasing God. There are thousands of ways you can serve God in this world, and you need to find the way that gives you the most satisfaction. This is very important to do when discerning your call. Talk with older, wiser, mature Christians about your call and how you might realize living your passion. Some may encourage you and some may discourage you, but you take the total of discussions you have had and decide what you have learned from them. This step of discernment is critical to your finding how to live your call. It is a slow process if you are diligent.

Ask the Spirit of Jesus to guide you in prayer. One way to do this may be by going on a retreat with a spiritual advisor. There are retreat centers all over the country and they are affordable and approachable. Ask people who have taken retreats about their experience and judge what would be a good fit for you. It is amazing how the Spirit works when you sacrifice a few days (or many days) to just pray and listen to God speaking to you.

Everyone is called. You are called. What do you want to do about it? Trust that God is not going to ask you to do anything that you would not love doing. God knows you better than you know yourself. With the help of other good Christians, you are going to find a life of love, joy, peace, hope and faith that you will never regret in this world or the next.

Sanctification

10
Sanctification

"The Spirit of the Lord is upon me, because he has anointed me to bring good news to the poor. He has sent me to proclaim relief to the captives and recovery of sight to the blind, to let the oppressed go free, to proclaim the year of the Lord's favor."

Luke 4:18 [NRSVA]

The word sanctification means holiness, and this is why we were born into this world – to become as holy as possible. We will never become perfectly holy in this world, but we will become perfect/holy in Heaven. This is why God created us, to be part of God's creative activity in the universe, and this will be explored further.

Holiness is absolutely essential to serving God. This is what I learned in my NDE. Because God is holy, only holy people can serve in intimate relationship with God. The Bible says that when we get to Heaven, we will become like Christ. (Romans 8:29, I John 3:2-3). Can you fully comprehend that statement? Do you, an imperfect being, believe that you will be like Christ? This is our ultimate destiny. To be part of God's creation forever. This is the opposite of self-righteousness. This holiness is to care about others more than oneself.

The ultimate experience in Heaven is to be in the presence of God. Nothing imperfect can be in the presence of God. Anyone with the slightest flaw would be so repelled by the power and love of a holy God that they would be cast away. Before the glory of God, we pour ourselves out in worship of God. One of the most difficult characteristics of Heaven is time as we know it does not exist there. Everything is present time. When we go to Heaven, we will have no anxiety about time because we will be so trusting in God's love. We will know our sanctification will be a process of love, joy, and peace. God's will is our salvation and we will know it.

A person who has achieved total sanctification is in awe of the overwhelming love and beauty of God. Many are just basking in that love immobile for long periods of time. Eventually, they want to participate in what is commonly called the Heavenly Choir. The Heavenly choir is not only continuously praising God, but they are also creating an energy that is part of all creation. If the Heavenly choir were to cease, much of the universe would cease to exist.

> **God the creator is always creating, and we become part of that process.**

Creation exists in the presence of God.

Sanctification

This information may be too much to grasp, but this is the ultimate explanation of why sanctification is so important. One who is holy will not only see God and be in the presence of God but will participate in the creation with Him. The Bible says you shall be higher than the angels. Angels are beings that were created to serve God and that is what they do.

We are God's children, and we have a higher calling. Because of our experience in this world, we have chosen and discerned good and evil. As a result of our life experience, we have unique creative gifts to bring to God. Each of us has something of value to bring to the creation. What an opportunity to do what we love to serve God and the creative activity of God. One of the most important things we must do in life is to use our gifts by discovering what our gifts are. These gifts are our passions; things that give us energy and purpose. Discover and use your gifts and be the beautiful, wonderful person God made you to be.

How do we become so perfectly holy? This is a process that takes as long as necessary and varies for each individual. The beginning of the process is our choice in this life to follow good over evil. This is really a hard test of our character. Christians pray "lead us not into temptation but deliver us from evil" (Matthew 6:13) in the Lord's Prayer. This is a gift Jesus gave us. We learn God's will and resist the opposition to God's will. It is a battle called spiritual warfare. We are in the fight of our lives, and it never ends in this world. Every time you think you can relax a new challenge comes into your life. It can be exhausting, but with the help and power of the Spirit of Christ, we can be victors. Never give up, and always rely on Jesus to give you the strength to continue to victory. With Jesus on your side, you will always win. We must stand in our faith (Ephesians 6).

When it is time to let go of this life we will be met by Jesus, relatives, and our angels and taken to Heaven. There are many levels of Heaven, and we will be taken to the level that suits our level of sanctification that we have achieved in our life. Obviously, a saintly person goes to a higher level than someone who has to struggle all their life to reject sin and has barely followed Jesus. God knows us better than we know ourselves. God is not deceived by our delusions of ourselves.

> **God judges by the heart and not by appearances.**
> (John 7:24)

Purification is what this process is all about. In the Catholic theology, this is called 'purgatory', which just means purification. When we go to Heaven, we are not magically made perfect. Just as our life has been a process of growth, learning, and transformation, so is our entry into the Heavenly realms. This process is not punishment, it is not torment, and it is not painful. This process is all about love, patience, and kindness. We progress at our own rate, and we gradually grow in sanctification with the help of God, our relatives, and the angels. It is a slow and gentle process that we will love as we progress in holiness. We have been given an incredible head start in this process because Jesus died for our sins. In asking Jesus to be our savior, our past sins are forgiven. This forgiveness Jesus gives us eradicates the sins we have repented, and our record is wiped clean. But we always have to deal with our shortcomings to be absolutely perfect in the light of a holy God.

People ask what we will do in Heaven, and the answer is that we will do whatever we want. If you want to rest in a meadow of flowers, you will. If you want to meet with the saints and talk, you can do this. If you want to sail a boat on the sea, you can do that. If you want to play the violin, you can do that. You can do anything you desire as long as it is good. Of course, you would never desire anything evil in Heaven because you have learned in this life not to do that. One way to think of our life in this world is to think of it as school and the curriculum is to know the love and goodness of God. We make choices every day and that is how we learn. This is called experiential learning, and is the most effective method according to experts.

> *We learn by our experiences and that is based on free will as we grow in wisdom and holiness.*

As we become more perfect, we move into more sanctified levels of Heaven with the goal of reaching the highest level, which is the presence of God. This love is impossible to describe because it is beyond words. It is far greater than anything we have known in our lives. Can you even imagine basking in the love of God who created you and wants you close to love you more? Sanctification takes time, and there is no time in Heaven because God's world is all in the present and not in the future or in the past. This is a really hard concept to grasp. In our worldly lives, we typically live in the past or in the future. This is one of the delusions of our earthly life because the past and the future are constructs of our mind and don't really exist. Only the present moment actually exists, and how many of us live in the moment? Do you really listen? Do you really see? Do you really feel? Are you living life in the Spirit? This is what we are talking about when we refer to living in the present. This is what it means to be holy, which is complete.

Every credible near-death experience says the same thing: it is all about love. The word 'love' is much abused and is often used to describe a fleeting emotion. The meaning of love in the Bible is the act of love. This can be summarized as caring about another person more than yourself (John 15:13). This is the real meaning of love, which is the unconditional love God gives. This is too often rarely known in our world. You can often see this love in a mother for her child. Do you know this love? Can you give this love?

In Heaven, you are always in the now, and it is a wholly new experience. We have so much to learn, and it is confusing to consider in this world, but in Heaven, we will always be in a state of bliss, which is being filled with the love of God. Do not doubt for a second your joy, peace, and faith in Heaven because the love of God will sustain you, and you could never want for anything more. Thanks be to God.

Community

11

Community

"Indeed, God did not send the son into the world to condemn the world, but in order that the world might be saved through him. Those who believe in him are not condemned; but those are condemned already, because they have not believed in the name of the only Son of God."

John 3:17-18 [NRSVA]

This chapter could be called church. My definition of church is a place where two or three are gathered in Jesus' name, but that may not be everyone's definition. The word church comes from the Greek word 'ecclesia', which means 'those called together'. When we use the word church, we are frequently referring to a specific building at a certain location, but there are home churches and churches that meet in rented locations, such as restaurants, empty commercial space, and hotels.

I spent twenty to thirty hours a week pastoring. This included people coming to my office with concerns. Much of my time was spent visiting members in hospitals and nursing homes and visiting shut-ins. I very much enjoyed doing these visits, but they were exhausting. These visits were a ministry of being present, listening intently, and offering prayer. After a few of these in an afternoon, I was wiped out. There is more suffering in the world than most people are aware of, and when you empathetically listen, you share in their suffering.

Worship preparation requires at least ten or twenty hours a week. Reading scriptures and commentaries and developing the worship for Sunday is challenging and fun. During worship, one has prayers, special music, responsive readings, and the sermon. These all need to be based on a theme, which is, in turn, based on the scriptures selected. I loved this part of the ministry. Sometimes of worship were better than others but you can't hit the ball out of the park every time you go up to bat. I retired from ministry in my seventies for health reasons. It was becoming painfully obvious to me that I was not able to do the job that I expected of myself, and I concluded that it was time to give it up. I occasionally still preach when invited, but I don't miss the constant demands and the sense of being exhausted.

> **"The church is a hospital for sinners, not a museum for saints."**
> – Abigail Van Buren

Church can be anywhere Christians gather. What is special about church and why do we need it? The early church in Rome met in underground tombs called the catacombs. Not very glamorous. A thousand years later, the church was building spectacular cathedrals.

Humans are social creatures, and they need and are dependent on one another. Civilization is a vast, complex social structure which humans have developed over the past ten thousand years and have prospered even to the point of overpopulation in many cities in the world. The fact is, we are completely dependent on each other. Even the frontiersmen who ventured into the unknown wilderness carried firearms they did not make. They were also packing other manufactured goods such as blankets, knives, and canteens. The horses had saddles and bridles that had been purchased. This complete dependency on each other extends today to the people who homestead. Their success or failure depends on having the necessary manufactured equipment. We are all completely dependent on one another. Thanks be to God for the water department, roads, electricity, and all the privileges of civilization that we take for granted.

The church is a most unusual universal community because it produces no material goods. The vast majority of communities are centered around a product or a service. **The closest organization to a church would be a hospital**. In fact, the comparison of a hospital to a church is intriguing. The biggest difference would be that hospitals are for the healing of the body in temporary visits, while the church is for spiritual healing and seeks to be a lifetime home away from home. Some churchgoers are involved in their church several days a week and it can be the most important part of their lives. For some people, church is a cultural tradition that has very little or marginal importance in their lives; they might attend church on Christmas or Easter.

The Christian church aspires to bring people together to grow in the Christian faith. Hopefully churches are presenting Jesus Christ as revealed in the Gospels and nothing more and nothing less. Regrettably, sometimes churches stray from the Gospel and become centered on other things. What is the role of politics in church? Is it destructive to be an institution that is open and inviting to all those people who have differing political opinions? As Jesus was inclusive in his ministry, the church must be inclusive. Jesus gave himself to often dealing with the lowest outcasts of society. He served and befriended lepers, prostitutes, women, idolaters, and Roman collaborators. He was despised by the self-righteous Jewish rulers of His county for these relationships. This was the very definition of inclusive vs. exclusive religion. What is your choice?

Far too often, the church becomes an exclusive club a stranger can clearly feel they are not part of. Most churches would deny this exclusive atmosphere, but if you visit various churches, you will definitely know where you are truly welcomed and where you are not. Taking this example to an extreme, how would a church welcome an extreme outsider such as a prostitute or a criminal? The answer is obvious that it would be a very rare church that would welcome such a person. How about people of different sexual preferences? Would they be welcomed? The development of the exclusive club mentality is contrary to the Gospel of Jesus Christ and damaging to the ministry of Christianity. How did Jesus treat the outsiders?

Ideally, the Christian community has wide open doors that are especially inviting to sinners. Since one of the fundamental teachings of the church is that we are all sinners and need a Savior, why do we decide to exclude a type of person who is different than our comfort zone? That is a serious challenge to the church, because when it has that mentality of serving its members by being comfortable and excluding anyone who disturbs the club's unwritten rules of who can belong, that church is betraying the Gospel. Humans are masters of self-deception. We too often betray our better instincts because of hidden desires, such as lust, greed, anger, revenge, and ego-centric needs. We can use the excuse of not knowing, but when we listen to our hearts, we do know not to abuse others.

People who don't go to church are often extremely prejudiced against the church. They have preconceived notions or negative experiences about the teaching, purpose, and motivation of the church. Since Christianity is all about bringing people into a relationship with God through Jesus Christ, what is the problem? Christians know and have experienced the fact that Christian faith gives one hope, joy, peace, and love. Why would anyone not want these gifts? The church is not about demeaning people and promoting guilt by putting people down. Regrettably, the church has done that too often, and there are millions of wounded people in our society who have had very negative experiences of church and will not go back. The church has a terrible reputation amongst a segment of society, especially those who have been wounded.

The power of the Christian faith is transforming lives by knowing and following Jesus. How do we get that message across to our culture, which is always selling things that we don't necessarily need or want. The church is not selling anything. The church is giving it away for free.

> *The love of God is priceless and far beyond any monetary considerations.*

That must be clearly communicated by the church. There is no hidden price tag to accepting Jesus as your Savior.

Ideally, the financial needs of the church will be conveyed to the members, and they will respond with generous donations. If this is not working to keep the institution solvent, then the solution is not guilt and shame to milk the congregation. Something is wrong, and that needs to be identified and resolved. Just one possible suggestion is if the church is actively pursuing ministries and actively supporting ministries, people will get enthusiastic and want to support the work of the church.

If the church does little but keep itself comfortable, really, who needs it? Why support a club for members only?

What does the church really do? There are several critical and different things that the church does. One, it is a place to change lives by presenting people with the opportunity to open their hearts, minds, and souls to the Spirit of Jesus Christ. This is commonly called getting saved. Some Christians use this term and others don't, but they are all after the same thing. Secondly, the church provides people with the opportunity to worship. Worship is not entertainment; it is glorifying God with praise. There are numerous styles of worship, and they are all good, it just depends on a person's cultural background and taste. Most people enjoy ice cream, but everyone has favorite flavors and flavors that they do not like. It is the same with worship styles. The important thing is giving people a time and place to praise God and make a connection with God. Thanks be to God that there is such a great diversity in church styles. We all need this in our lives.

Thirdly, the church is the creator, and supporters of ministries that may be within the confines of the church but also may reach out into the community and reach out into the whole world. How exciting is it for a church to support an overseas ministry. The Bible says that the purpose of the church is "to equip the saints for ministries." (Ephesians 3:3). The Bible also says:

"Go therefore and make disciples of all nations, baptizing them in the name of the Father and of the Son and of the Holy Spirit, and teaching them to obey everything that I have commanded you."
Matthew 28:19-20 [NRSVA]

The church was not called together to be a country club of self-satisfied and comfortable people. It was called to be open to everybody so that they would really know Jesus and take him into the world.

What's not to love about the church? If it is alive and has enthusiasm for doing ministry, it is so appealing and so irresistible.

The Way, The Truth and The Life | 130

Community

Engaging every member to be part of the ministry according to their capabilities gives the church life. Think on the woman who demonstrates hospitality by making food and coffee, or the Sunday School teacher who nurtures faith in all ages. Thanks be to God for those who go out into the world and build houses for the poor or who care for the poor with food and clothes. What is not to love about the community of Christians we call church? When the church is alive, it does ministries that draw people into participation and thrive.

Something happened in 2001 that really changed my life. I went on a mission trip to Belize, Central America, with a group to serve. We were taken to a faraway village called San Victor, which was populated with Mayan and Maya-Mestizo people. I witnessed poverty that I had never imagined. Most of the people lived in houses made of stick walls, thatched roofs, and dirt floors. Some of these homes were inhabited by twelve or eighteen people. There was no furniture, and the people slept in hammocks, several in each hammock. There was no electricity, no telephones, no cars, no bicycles, no toilets, and almost no possessions. It was shocking to an American who considers these things necessities. Strangely, these were the happiest, most decent people I have ever met. Not all of them were saints, but I fell in love with these people.

After this mission trip in 2001, I immediately made plans and organized another mission trip back to San Victor, Belize, that year. In twenty-two years, I took hundreds of people on thirty mission trips to San Victor. We helped build most of the school buildings, plus seventy-six houses, a big Catholic church, and a grand community center. We also helped send hundreds of young people to high school and college. We had health clinics, got people free operations, and, most importantly, built relationships.

We saw the Spirit of Christ in them and tried to show the Spirit of Christ in us. This mission work became the passion of my life and continues to this day. This ministry of hundreds of people making the sacrifice of time and work has dramatically changed lives for the people we served and for the missionaries. Mission work is transformative.

Your Gifts

12

Your Gifts

"We know that all things work together for good for those who love God, who are called according to his purpose. For those whom he foreknew he also predestined to be conformed to the image of his Son, in order that he might be the first born within a large family."

Romans 8:28-29 [NRSVA]

Your gifts are who you are, and even more importantly, your gifts are your contribution to God's creation. We were created to be part of God's plan for the world and the universe. That is what this chapter is about. You are no accident of birth because God made you for a purpose. This is why Jesus says in the scriptures when we go to Heaven, "Well done, good and faithful servant. Enter into my kingdom" (Matthew 25:23).

Your purpose in life is to serve God's purpose with the gifts you have been given. An obvious example would be a woman who has always wanted to get married and have children. She is a devoted mother, and then later, an engaged and wonderful grandmother upon whom her children rely. This is her life, and she is using the gifts she was born with and doing what she wanted to do with her life's gifts. We all know of women like this, and we usually take them for granted, sometimes even demeaning them. No matter how we dismiss them, they are doing God's will by using their gifts.

> **There is nothing in this world as important as raising children, and these women are welcomed into Heaven as "good and faithful servants."**

So, what about the rest of us who are living and using our gifts for God's purpose? You have probably known people who have said "I don't know what I want to do." Have you known people who say, "I know what I want to do but there is no way I can do it because I have to keep the job I hate"? Do you know people who say, "I think I would like to do this, but maybe I would be better at that"? Discerning your gifts and then living those gifts is what it is all about. Have you ever met a man or woman who has said "I love my job"? This is a life well spent and that person is serving God whether they know it or not.

Can you become the person who says, "I love my job"? Don't imagine that you have to sell all of your worldly possessions and move to the jungle of Borneo to serve as a missionary to serve God's purpose. Your gift may be to work as a plumber and to love your work. Interestingly, plumbers make a good living in our society. How are plumbers doing God's will? Just consider how absolutely important plumbing is to our civilization. Sanitation, waste disposal, hygiene, clean water, and warm showers are what plumbers give us, and thanks be to God, we all take this for granted. The next time you are enjoying that warm shower, give thanks to God for the plumber who made it possible. You needn't do something spectacular to serve God, live your purpose, and have a wonderful life.

If you are searching for your gifts, start with what you love to do and what you do not love to do. Be clear in your mind about your passion. For some, this is easy, and for others, this is confusing. It is important to do this and discover what you love, what you enjoy, and what you hate. Keep narrowing this down until there is a specific set of gifts that you want to exercise in your life. Then, the next step is to figure out a way to do this for a living. Does your chosen career require a certain education? If you have chosen to be a doctor, there is a long and expensive set of requirements, but it is doable. If you want to be an athlete, what do you need to do, and are there opportunities to use your gift? What if you don't meet the standards of an individual athlete? What about becoming a coach of the sport you love? The point is to find a way to live your gift. Then you will have a happy and fulfilling life and be serving God. Doing a job you hate and being miserable is not a good life, and you will miss using the gifts that God has given you. One only gets one chance of living in this world. Don't squander it.

You are told to be happy in your work, but that is not easy to do if you hate or are indifferent to what you are doing. In a free society, there are endless opportunities to find your perfect career. There may be many reasons why it is hard to get there, but if this is what you were gifted to do, with the help of God, you will find a way. How fortunate are we who live in free societies where we can follow our gifts and passions. Contrastingly, it is hard to live in a closed society where one has very little freedom to choose, but God will guide you. Do the research and talk to people in the field you are seeking to become a part of. Those doing it know how to get there and are usually eager to share what they know. If you are certain and pursue it, you will attain a fulfilling life.

Let's look at one way of using your gifts that a few persons feel called to, and that involves serving the church. People mistakenly think that the highest calling is to be a priest or pastor. It is not the 'highest calling'. It is just a very specific calling.

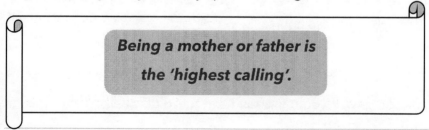

Being a mother or father is the 'highest calling'.

It is a position that gets recognition and carries plenty of responsibility. It requires serious self-sacrifice and time. Giving birth to a child and raising them well is exceedingly pleasing to God. Becoming a successful politician and having power and wealth may be pleasing or not to God depending on what you do. God values the bricklayer as much as the farmer.

> **God loves the farmer as much as the billionaire.**

Working for the church has many opportunities, like being a youth minister, serving as church administrator, doing mission work, working in evangelism, performing as a musician, and pastoring. How important is a gifted musician to worship? The answer is invaluable. How important is a competent and kind person as a church administrator to the running of a church? Their worth is beyond words. Children and youth are the future of the church and the world, and those who minister to them are doing an extremely important job. **Sunday School teachers and youth leaders change lives.** Like any call, it requires discernment, research, and wise counsel.

Being a pastor is a very special calling and requires a set of specific gifts. If you think you have these gifts, talk to your pastor and others to get their honest assessment as to whether you possess these gifts. The majority of people who pursue going into the ministry drop out because, at some point, they realize it is not for them. It would be best if a person did a lot of soul searching and talking to pastors about their experiences before they go after it. It is not as glamorous and a lot harder than people know. This is also true for any profession or life's work.

God wants you to use your gifts and be joyful in your life.

May We All Be One

13

May We All Be One

"I ask not only on behalf of these, but also on behalf of those who will believe in me through their word, that they may all be one."

John 17:20-21 [NRSVA]

Jesus prayed "Holy Father, protect them in your name that you have given me, so that they may be one, as you and I are one." (John 17:11 [NRSVA]). The Christian Church has clearly ignored this verse and others just like it over the past two thousand years. **One of the serious problems with Christianity today is not its diversity; it is the animosity expressed by Christians towards one another of different denominations and points of view.** Christians clearly don't appreciate how much this infighting destroys our credibility to the unbelievers. It is readily apparent to the doubters that since they can't agree, why should we take them seriously? This gives the unbelievers a strong argument for dismissing Christianity. Christians need to respect fellow believers and differences in non-essentials.

How can Christians agree when they have different points of view? First of all, professionals in every field, whether it is law, medicine, science, academia, politics, etc., disagree all the time until there is a general consensus. For example, geologists thought the theory of continental shift was completely crazy when it was first proposed. After decades of controversy, it was finally accepted as a scientific fact. Today, all geologists officially subscribe to the theory of continental drift. Closer to home, the atomic theory that was taught in school in the 1960s is not what passes for scientific truth today. What was true science a few years ago is no longer true. The reality of science is changing all the time. Medicine is changing all the time. The legal system is very erratic. Politics is maddening. What is true and unchanging in this world?

The Bible doesn't change, and it has been speaking truth for thousands of years. The Bible is full of hope, praise, and love. Why are we not focused on the truths of the Bible and especially on Jesus Christ, as opposed to nonessentials? Is the method of baptism really worth being divided about? **Denominations separate over the most trivial things, but behind it all is power and control.** Humans are a contradiction between the need to join in wide social bonds like a country and the need to be tribal. The command of God that we read in the prayer of Jesus is "on behalf of those who will believe in me through their word, that they may all be one." (John 17:21 [NRSVA]). What don't we understand about these words? How can we have the absolutely wonderful diversity of worship and expression of faith that we have in the world today and create unity. If you have visited different kinds of churches, you will discover the Christian faith expressed in a variety of ways. Some congregations are openly emotional and lively, and some congregations are very formal and reserved. Some congregations have 'high church' and some congregations have 'low church'. Is this not wonderful? Go to the church that meets your needs. This is not a threat to anyone. **The threat to the Christian Church is tribalism, which means thinking that we are right, and our way is superior to another's way.** We are incompatible because we cannot respect you, your traditions, and style of worship. What is this?

Jesus Christ, the Gospels, and the Christian faith is the foundation unchanging for two thousand years. Why do we have thousands of disappearing churches that not only do not respect one another but that are actually antagonistic to their brothers and sisters in Christ?

The following are suggestions for what we must do to stop this terrible state of sin that we are engaging in by rejecting the word of God. Let us begin by building bridges with our fellow Christians in the communities we live in. We can have fellowship with one another and even have shared worship experiences. In fellowship, we can learn to love and respect each other. Just because a person has different tastes doesn't mean we can't love them. Everyone in our family has different tastes and we love them as they are.

> *One of the greatest ways of working together is mission work.*

What are the needs in our community and the surrounding area? How can we cooperate to reach out to the community? Can a food pantry be better by working together? Can the needs of the elderly and disabled be identified and addressed by working cooperatively? There are endless ways churches can be more effective by working together. It is a shame this so rarely done; it only makes sense to do so.

Jesus Christ is far more important than tribalism, which is based on fear and egotism. The individual churches must reach out to their brothers and sisters in Christ and build unity. No one has to give up their style of worship and no one has to give up control of their form of government. We can thrive in a state of mutual love and cooperation while keeping our own autonomy. What an amazingly different world of Christianity this would be in the future. It costs nothing but letting go of tribalism and embracing Jesus Christ as our Lord and Savior.

Imagine making the essentials of the Christian faith supreme in our motivation and actions. What a different face of Christianity we would present to the world. How wonderful that the church over there has loud rock music in worship while another church has a very quiet and formal liturgy, and yet another church has very casual services. Think of these differences as a variety of flowers in the garden of God giving glory to God. Lifting up Jesus Christ is the reason for our existence.

One of my passions has been mission work. I worked for years as a volunteer of an inner-city mission church and ran a Saturday lunch program for six years that fed between two-hundred and four-hundred people. For eleven years, I oversaw the food pantry in our town that fed three to four hundred lunches a month. It was a pleasure for me to serve the poor and needy.

Good and Faithful Servant

14

Good and Faithful Servant

"It is no longer I who live, but it is Christ who lives in me. And the life I now live in the flesh I live by faith in the Son of God, who loved me and gave himself for me."

Galatians 2:20 [NRSVA]

Jesus said, "Good and faithful servant, enter into my kingdom." These are exactly the words we want to hear when we have died and Jesus has come to meet us. Being a good and faithful servant means that we have lived our life serving God to the best of our ability. It never says that being perfect is a requirement for going to Heaven. The Bible says we should strive for perfection, which is sanctification. Jesus died on the cross to cover and erase our sins. Serving Jesus does not mean that we have to drop out of society and become a recluse. Jesus describes what a follower of His does.

Jesus and I had a very long argument during my near-death experience. I wanted to stay forever in Heaven, and He patiently explained to me why I had to come back to this world. He told me that I "didn't have the character to fit into Heaven and I needed to live my life in the way he showed me so that I would be suitable for Heaven."

In Matthew 25: 31-46, there is a long passage describing the kinds of things his followers do. Part of it is addressed to those who got it right.

"Truly, I tell you, just as you did it to one of the least of these who are members of my family, you did it to me."

Matthew 25: 40 [NRSVA]

This is open to a wide range of interpretation, and you may respond however the Holy Spirit guides you. The busy attorney can find multiple ways of helping the downtrodden, the mother's life is completely filled with caring for 'the least of these' (her children), and the production manager has an opportunity to insist that his employees are treated fairly and well cared for. Everyone has the opportunity to treat every single person in their little world with kindness, compassion, and caring.

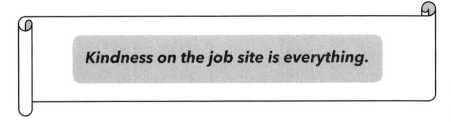

Kindness on the job site is everything.

This territory of living the way of Jesus covers our family, our neighbors, our coworkers, our country, and the world. That's a lot of ground, but what can we do about it? The truth is, we can only do our tiny little part with the resources we have achieved in life.

This means you visit your aunt in the hospital when she is sick, and you visit her when she goes home. You make sure she has the care she needs to recover. You give a child a ride to school whose single parent can't get them there. You can help to feed the poor by working at a food pantry or a kitchen that feeds the poor. You do what you can, when you can. What is a good and faithful servant? This is a person who responds with kindness and caring whenever or wherever the opportunity arises. Loving the person you are with.

People who are in the medical field, those who are teachers, and persons who provide social services are fortunate because these vocations provide the perfect opportunity to serve others in the way of Jesus. Others may wonder if they have that opportunity. Absolutely. We all are given this opportunity daily in how we interact with the people around us. What we do is important, and how we do it is just as important. The critical thing is doing things with kindness, such as having genuine love and interest in the persons we work with. What it comes down to is seeing the Christ in everyone we meet.

> **The Spirit of Christ is in everyone, not just those who go to church.**

If you approach people by searching for the Christ in them, you will usually find it. In doing prison ministry, what is surprising is all the good one finds in people who have committed felonies. When you listen to their stories, theirs is a world of really bad choices that deceived them into thinking these were the best possible choices. Discussing their history, they can discover better ways to get along in the world different from what their past environment showed them. They have been deceived by a corrupt world.

Being a good and faithful servant is an active, full-time life of having good intentions. This means we do not seek to save people, because only God can do that. We cannot fix people or change them because only they can do that. Our interaction is to model the Spirit of Christ and help them find that Spirit in themselves. It is there if we can encourage it. How wonderful if we have the chance to lead a person to accepting Jesus as their Savior and Lord. Always remember, it is the power of God working and not us doing anything except trying to be good and faithful servants.

In this life, we will encounter many obstacles, disappointments, and deceptions. The power of evil hates us and will attempt anything and everything to defeat and hinder us from doing good. We have to stand firm in our faith and be strong in the full armor of God. It is critically important that we know Ephesians 6:10-18 because this describes in simple and graphic terms how we stand firm in our faith and defend ourselves from the assault of the evil forces around us.

"...be strong in the Lord and in the strength of his power. [...] Pray in the Spirit at all times in every prayer and supplication. To that end keep alert and always persevere in supplication for all the saints."

Ephesians 6:10-18 [NRSVA]

We are in a battle to be good and faithful servants. Wouldn't it be nice if we lived in a perfect world? Heaven on Earth is not here yet, but it will happen someday, we just don't know when. For now, we just do our best. We struggle within ourselves to be more holy in every thought, word, and deed. We struggle to follow the guidance of the Spirit of Christ to lead us in our activities, and we battle the forces of evil that are trying to defeat us. We will be victors with Jesus as our strength.

The best way is to have as much support as you possibly can. This means having friends that are on the same page as you. Hopefully you can find fellow Christians that get you and your struggle. You need to cultivate these relationships with people who will stand by you. It is also really important to have the nourishment of regular worship. Worship gets your battery charged. Find that place with that worship that enlivens you and strengthens your faith. Lastly, a strong and regular prayer life keeps us in touch with the Spirit of Christ and enables us to stand firm in our faith and serve God.

When we die, we will go to Heaven or Hell. If we are going to Heaven, the Bible says that Jesus and the angels will come and take us to Heaven, where we will be greeted by all the long-lost relatives and friends who are in Heaven. It will be the happiest day of our life. John 14:3 says, "And if I go and prepare a place for you, I will come again and will take you to myself, so that where I am, there you may be also." [NRSVA].

Heaven on Earth

15

Heaven on Earth

"This is my commandment, that you love one another as I have loved you. No one has greater love than this, to lay down one's life for one's friends."

John 15:12-13 [NRSVA]

There is life after death, and this has been experienced by millions of people all over the world who have testified to their experiences. There are hundreds of books of testimonies and hundreds more testimonies of near-death experiences on the internet. This topic is not new. In fact, there are near-death experiences (NDEs) recorded going back several thousand years. NDEs lost credibility in the age of enlightenment because they were about supernatural things that were being discredited. Science has not found a way to prove or disprove NDEs, so there is no scientific proof they happen. The millions of NDE testimonies are considered anecdotal evidence, which is not very scientific. There is no known way to prove by testing a person dying and having these NDEs. That does not invalidate the experiences of millions of people globally.

Very recently, scientists who study the brain have announced that the mind exists independent of the brain, and they have come to this conclusion scientifically. This supports the possibility that NDEs are valid experiences of life after death. The whole subject was opened up to discussion when Raymond Moody wrote his book 'Life after Death', which was published in 1975 and became a bestseller. Since then, there has been an explosion of interest in the subject of NDEs.

If you want a glimpse into Heaven, you can research what these NDEs say about Heaven and Heaven on Earth. This author had an NDE in 1985 and has talked to hundreds of NDE experiencers, read many books, and listened to many testimonies in the past almost forty years.

Every authentic NDE states emphatically that love is the basis of what God is and what God wants to be our primary motivation. This love is not sentimental or superficial; rather, it is what determines our every choice and action. As Jesus said in John 13: 34, this is my commandment: "Love one another as I have loved you." [KJ21]. This is what Heaven on Earth will be like. Everyone on the globe will be loving one another. Can you imagine what that would look like? It is such a radically different human society and culture that it challenges the imagination, but I have been given a preview of this Heaven on Earth and will briefly share what I have learned with you of what I saw.

Jesus took me to a village of people living in total harmony with themselves and with the natural environment. The critical word is 'harmony'. Like an orchestra works in harmony because they all share a common objective and have a conductor to meet that objective, so it will be with Heaven on Earth. To continue the analogy, the score everyone is following is provided by the Holy Spirit, which is the Spirit of God and the Spirit of Christ. That Spirit is universal, and it always has been universal in the world, but sadly, it is often ignored and even opposed by other spirits. Heaven on earth will be ruled by God's love. Opposition to this love will cease and the power of God's love will be in everyone globally.

In the village, everyone cared for the welfare of everyone else. Everybody had their individual work to do to contribute for themselves and to share with everyone else. Some people farmed, some people built, some people manufactured things, some people taught, and some people prayed. **Everyone was equally important. There was no hierarchy because everyone admired the talents and abilities of everyone else.** From the least to the greatest, they were all respected for their individual gifts. Each was nurtured in their unique gifts.

The primary work of the whole community was the raising of children. The families lived in their own homes with the children, but every person in that community interacted with the children as if they were the parent of that child. There is a saying today that 'it takes a village to raise a child'. This has always been true.

When Heaven on Earth comes, this will be a reality. Psychologists say much of our personality is formed by the age of eight years. How many of us have been deeply traumatized by incidents in our early childhood. When Heaven on earth comes, all will have a perfect childhood based in love. The opposition to God's love will not exist. This battle against God's love is called evil and that will cease. The power of love will prevail, especially in child-rearing.

Each individual will be nurtured to discover and develop their unique gifts and contribute those gifts to the community. For example, if a child has a passion for music, that will be encouraged. If a child has a passion for woodworking, that will be encouraged. Each individual has a passion for something, and that will be encouraged and taught by the person in the community who has that same passion with years of experience in that field. So somewhere in that child's development, their unique gifts are identified, and they become 'apprenticed' to an expert in that particular field. They still live with their family but spend most of the day with the master learning.

If an individual's level of achievement exceeded the village's ability to teach them, they left the village for another to further their learning. Every village was known for its exceptional and unique talents and these gifts were shared among villages. This meant that one village was exceptional for scientific research and development, another village was advanced in architectural development, another village was well known for music. and another was leading in textiles. These villages shared and traded all the time.

This description of one little part of Heaven on earth is only a fragment of what I was shown. The future of the entire planet is not very different from the rule of God's love and how that is manifested in the future. When this will happen, no one knows. How we will get there depends on humanity changing radically. This is God's will and that means it is coming. The question is whether it will come peacefully or are there going to be catastrophes that will force humanity to change.

The hope is that we will work for a peaceful conversion of the heart for all humankind. That is God's plan for us.

When We Get to Heaven

16

When We Get to Heaven

"For now we see in a mirror, dimly, but then we will see face to face. Now I know only in part; then I will know fully, even as I have been fully known."

1 Corinthians 13:12 [NRSVA]

Jesus told me the biggest difficulty people have when they die is not knowing they have died because it feels wonderful. In the process of the body dying, there is typically plenty of pain and suffering. That is all gone when a person dies. In fact, they feel better than they have ever felt in their life. Jesus, with the angels and saints who have come to escort them to Heaven, have to convince them that they have not been healed, their body is dead, and they are going to Heaven. Letting go of this earthly world is challenging for some people. We are in the process of adapting to our Heavenly body.

The amazing thing about this process is that Jesus comes and gets us in the dying process. The other wonderful thing is we can still carry the illusion that we are in our earthly body. This is an illusion that is subtly changed as we are transformed into our eternal bodies.

> *The imperishable external body is made of pure energy that can appear in ordinary human form or take on another, more beautiful appearance.*

We are always still ourselves in every way except that we can choose to be young and beautiful, which everyone chooses eventually. **This process of accepting the spiritual body is at the rate a person chooses.**

The greeting committee includes persons we loved and who are familiar to us. These reunions are our introduction to the love of Heaven. It is all quite emotionally overwhelming. This is all preparation for us coming into the love of God, which permeates everything in Heaven. The love of God is everywhere and in everything.

We will be taken to the level of Heaven that is appropriate for our degree of spiritual development. There are countless levels of Heaven, and they are seamless. As we increase in sanctification, we will move closer and closer to the Heavenly choir and the presence of God. Some levels are more therapeutic for our rehabilitation. Other levels are for those who have achieved a higher level of sanctification in this earthly life. Our earthly life was a gift for us to choose between loving God with all our heart, mind, and strength and loving our neighbor as ourselves or rejecting God's love and doing what we want to do. Those who have rejected God's love are not going to Heaven. The only people in Heaven are those who have some degree of love of God and who have tried to live by it. Those who have rejected God go on a very different path.

When we get to Heaven, we are all in need of some degree of purification, and we will receive that with compassion and patience before we move up to the Heavenly realm. There is no time in Heaven, so this process of purification may happen relatively quickly or it may be a long process. It doesn't make any difference because time is irrelevant. The whole point is to let go of the dross and become refined as pure love. We never lose our good qualities of character; we simply let go of the things that are undesirable. Eventually, we will go into the very presence of God, but we must be perfect to do that.

Everything good that God has created is in Heaven; therefore, Heaven is vast beyond comprehension. Are there oceans in Heaven, forests, gardens, buildings, deserts, mountains, roads, cities, and loving people? Yes, to all of these and everything God has made. Our dwelling place depends on what level of Heaven we have deserved. Of course, we don't need any building to dwell in because the weather in Heaven is always beautiful daytime. The buildings in Heaven are expressions of the love of God. There are many dwelling places in Heaven.

When we go to Heaven, we can explore, rest, question, play, and learn. Whatever we think we need, we can do within reason. Because of the ever-present love of God, we are drawn by that love toward God and purification. Our real life begins then. This is the life we were created for. Our purpose in our life, both on Earth and in Heaven, is to love God fully and to love one another as we love ourselves. This takes more than a lifetime, so no one ever achieves perfection on Earth, but some come closer than others.

Anyone who has sought sanctification in their journey in the world knows it is long and frustrating and filled with frequent setbacks. The Heavenly process is much smoother. **One of the serious obstacles we have about thinking of Heaven is we project our earthly life onto it, and they are not the same at all.** As spiritual beings, we are not the same either. Don't project earthly experience on Heaven; they are completely different worlds.

One of the greatest experiences in Heaven is meeting soul to soul with another person, and this is an intense experience unlike anything we know from earthly life. It gives a whole new meaning to falling in love. Of course, we will know our spouse(s), parents, and children in Heaven. but we will not have the same attachment to them that we had in our worldly life. We will have the love for many, just as we loved them. We will be delighted in how much they have transformed as loving and spiritual beings in the time we missed them. We will also pray for the people that have not come to Heaven. Possibly, in God's mercy, they will change in the realm that they have gone to. There is always the hope that they will change and turn their lives over to Jesus.

In Heaven, there are constant, new adventures leading to new understanding and personal growth. There is never any boredom or lack of something to do. One will never be lacking love and hope because you will be filled with love, hope, and faith.

The ultimate goal of everyone who goes to Heaven is to enter into the presence of God, the source of love and creation. No one dares go close to God who is not perfect in every way. God is surrounded by an enormous multitude of beings who are praising God, each in their own way. This Heavenly choir is doing more than just praising God; they are contributing to the energy, the vibration state that is the basic element of all creation. Some beings, after praising God, are called to rule over parts of the creation with angels as their army. **If the Heavenly choir were to cease, much of creation would disappear.**

The Way, The Truth and The Life | 164

When we get to Heaven, real life begins. From the struggles of our earthly existence, we are born into the life that we were created from the beginning to live forever.

> **The choices we make now determine whether we go to Heaven or not.**

The First Step

17

The First Step

"'Look,' he said, 'I see the heavens opened and the Son of Man standing at the right hand of God!'"

Acts 7:56 [NRSVA]

This chapter is a guide to finding salvation. If you are already on the way to sanctification or if you have been alienated from God, this can be helpful in getting on the right path. Salvation or getting saved comes from the Greek word rescue. Think of a person drowning in the ocean being approached by a boat that throws them a line to pull them aboard. This world is full of deceptions, distractions, and false promises. We can drown in this ocean of lies. The way, the truth, and the life of Jesus Christ as revealed in the Gospels is the only certain path to Heaven. This is the lifeline of salvation.

Jesus was asked how to attain eternal life (Mark 10:17-19, Luke 10:25-28). Jesus answered "Love God with all your heart, mind, and strength. Love your neighbor as yourself." This is the way he showed us in his life, his self-sacrifice on the cross, and his resurrection. Jesus lived this truth, demonstrated this with his life, and came into this world so that all might be saved and go to Heaven. As you know, some became his disciples, some became his followers, and some became his murderers. We are free to choose the way of Jesus or to reject it. That decision is the most important decision of your life. Trust and obey is the only way.

The first step is to recognize you need a Savior. At some point in your life, you are desperate enough to ask for help. You have tried everything to make yourself happy and fulfilled and everything you tried led to disappointment. Whatever you thought you knew, it is the moment to seek a higher power, God (the creator). Try calling on Jesus, who was sent into the world specifically to save you and me. There is power in the name of Jesus. Find out for yourself. No matter how many times you may have used the name of Jesus in an irreverent way, when you say it from the heart, you will get a response, if you are desperate enough. Pray always.

When you have had an emotional experience of Jesus' love for you, you have just begun the journey.

As the old saying goes, the journey of a thousand miles begins with the first step.

It happens that people have a powerful experience of the divine and then think they are enlightened and go their own way to and fro. **We rely on maps and GPS much in the way that Jesus is the map leading to a right relationship with God and the way to Heaven.** Wandering around following your own desires is guaranteed to keep you lost. Begin by reading the Bible and begin with the Gospels of Mathew, Mark, Luke, and John. Read slowly, little bits at a time, asking the guidance of the Holy Spirit. When you are well acquainted with the Gospels, read the rest of the New Testament. Then read the Hebrew Bible looking for where it is consistent with Jesus' teaching and where it is not. It is intelligent to look at the Bible critically and wrestle with what you find.

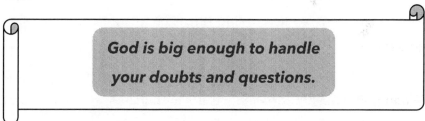

God is big enough to handle your doubts and questions.

Along with acquainting yourself with Jesus, begin to search for a community (a church, for example) that proclaims and worships the Jesus you have found. The key is a church that teaches love. If you go to a place that is focused on fear, demeaning other groups, or controlling its members, never go back. They are misusing the Christian faith by misrepresenting the Gospel of Jesus Christ. If you find the worship and the music uplifting, that is always a good sign. Remember, church is not entertainment. You go to church to worship God and to expand your understanding of God. An added benefit is that you are in a community of saints and sinners. The whole range of spiritual development is represented by that collection of people called Christians. Some are wiser than you, some are just beginning their faith journey (like you), and some are having real anger issues and are destructive (hopefully not like you). The people in church are a mixed bag. Seek out the mature Christians and avoid the hypocrites. You shall know them by their fruits. Mature Christians are engaged in some ministry or mission because that is what real Christians do. You shall know them by their fruits.

We have suggested first calling on Jesus to come into your life, secondly reading the Bible beginning with the Gospels, and thirdly finding a church that preaches love and has inspiring worship. The last suggestion is to find a ministry or mission through your life or church that meets your passions and abilities. There is a vast range of opportunities in any church large or small.

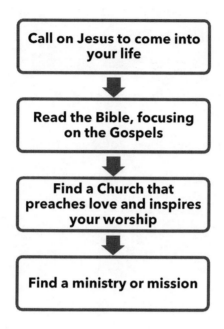

The following are just a few possibilities in the church to serve Jesus. Could you volunteer to usher, greet visitors, or serve coffee and cake during social time? These are all very important ministries that make the church inviting and growing. Does your church have a food pantry or participate in one where you could serve? Is there a ministry of serving food to the poor at your church? Do people go out into the community and help the elderly or poor with home maintenance? Do they participate in building houses for the poor? Have you the gifts to teach Sunday School? There is nothing more important than introducing children to the Christian faith. Is there a Bible study group you can join to grow and contribute your experiences with others who are on the same path? These are just a few suggestions; you will find your sweet spot in church.

Pray always. God loves you. God sent Jesus to show you the way. The Holy Spirit is there to guide you. The church is your path to true faith. You have everything you need to go to Heaven.

The Author

Here is a brief autobiography of the man who wrote this book. It is important to me that you know that I am no better or worse than you. My life has been several times in the valley of death and several times on the mountain top. The majority of my life has been spent just living like anyone else. There is nothing spectacular about my life. I am not famous or wealthy. My wife and I get by, and hope not to outlive our resources.

My parents both worked. My father was a salesman, and my mother was a nurse. My dad served in the navy during World War II as a lieutenant in naval air supply in New Guinea. My mother said he came back from the war a completely changed man. It was not for the good. Their marriage was very unhappy, but neither would consider divorce. I was their third child, born in 1946. They loved my two older sisters, but I was the boy they wanted. Growing up, my mother did her best to love me and spoil me. My father treated me as a low-grade soldier and ordered me around. Our relationship during my growing years went from bad to worse. I loved my saintly mother and hated my very emotionally and physically abusive father.

When I was a child, I drowned in the ocean and was resuscitated by my mother on the beach. I remember this incident vividly. After being underwater for longer than I could bear, I took a deep breath of sea water and was then surrounded by a brilliant white light and had an overpowering feeling of love and peace. When my mother resuscitated me, I was confused as to why she was crying because I had just had the most wonderful experience.

My family took us to church on Sunday, often just dropping us off. I loved the church, especially Sunday School. When I became a teenager, I was active in youth program and attended church. I took it seriously. I was baptized at the age of twelve, by my request. My pastor and I became close, and he told me I had a call to ministry. I was seriously considering this.

At the age of fifteen I asked the pastor (who was a graduate of Harvard Divinity School) if we could have a private meeting. At the meeting, I asked him many questions about what we "really believed" and he answered me that almost everything in the Christian faith was based on myths and superstition. I never went to church or saw the pastor again. I was totally disillusioned with Christianity and religion in general. My life became focused on my passion, which was painting. I was also attracted to existentialism and atheism.

After high school, my father would not pay for me to study art, so I was on my own. I got married, and after a failed attempt at reconciliation with my father, we moved from Massachusetts to San Francisco. I went there to study art at the San Francisco Art Institute. I worked as a waiter from 10 P.M. until 4 or 5 A.M. and I went to school from 9 A.M. to 4 P.M. My wife was a waitress at the same restaurant working from 5 P.M. to 9 P.M. We had our first child, a girl, and never used babysitters. When I graduated from the San Francisco Art Institute in 1968, I went to graduate school at the University of California, Berkeley. There I got my Master of Arts. and then my Master of Fine Arts.

After graduating in 1972, I was fortunate to find a job as a professor of art at a (then) new university in Northern Kentucky. Teaching and making art to exhibit became the focus of my life. All of my friends were fellow professors, and we were all hardcore atheists. At the bars on Saturday night, we checked out the ladies and made jokes about Christians. My family was secondary to my career.

In 1985, I took a group of art students around Europe. While there, on June 1st, 1985 at 11 A.M., I had a rupture of the duodenum that dropped me to the floor in terror and the most acute pain. My wife called the hotel desk, and they called an ambulance. I was taken to the emergency room of a hospital in Paris and examined.

There I was told that I would die within an hour or two if I did not have surgery. I was rushed to the surgical hospital and parked in a room. I was given no medicine and never saw a doctor for over ten hours. The pain, which had knocked me to the floor, intensified. At 8:30 P.M., I could not breathe anymore, and I said goodbye to my wife. I went unconscious and soon awoke standing in the room more aware than I have ever been. A group of people came to me outside the room and told me to come with them. I followed them on a long walk-in increasing darkness into Hell. Without going into too much detail, these people physically tore me apart. The pain was excruciating. By that time, I knew that I had left the world and that this was my fate forever. Laying in total darkness surrounded by exceedingly cruel people, I searched for a way out. Eventually, I vividly remembered being in Sunday School as a child and singing 'Jesus Loves Me'. I wanted this to be true and called out to Jesus. To my complete astonishment, Jesus came. He embraced me, loved me, and made me whole. Jesus took me to Heaven, and together with a group of angels, I was given a life review. When it was finished, He asked me if I had any questions. I asked Jesus every question I could think of, and He answered everything patiently and clearly. I cannot explain how wonderful this was. Then Jesus sent me back to this world for a second chance at life. I returned to my bed in the Paris surgical hospital. A doctor was finally located, and I had surgery beginning that night after 10 P.M. By that time, my life had been completely transformed by Jesus.

I was somehow able to tolerate a flight back to the United States a week after surgery and subsequently spent the next several months in a local hospital battling sepsis. After several months in the local hospital, I was finally able to go home. I was eager to go to church, and although I could barely walk at the time, my wife and I did go. When I entered the church, the congregation was singing 'A Mighty Fortress is our God'. I knew then that this was where I wanted to be, praising God and Jesus in worship, participating in prayer, and being engrossed in the sermons.

When I had further recuperated from my acute sepsis, I returned to the university as chairman of the art department. Meanwhile, I spent every spare moment at church volunteering for anything. After several years, I knew I was being called to full-time ministry, so I left the university and went to seminary. I served churches for three years as a guest pastor, or student pastor. I graduated from seminary in 1992 with a Master of Divinity degree and served as pastor of an inner-city church in Norwood, Ohio for fourteen years, followed by a church in West Central Ohio for six years, and finally a church in northern Kentucky for three years before my retirement.

I loved being a pastor and I continue to make artwork. I have been married three times and currently have the wife I have always dreamed of. There have been some very serious health problems recently, which I have overcome, to a degree. My two dogs and my wife and I have a beautiful life. My whole life since my near-death experience has been to testify about Jesus, who is the best friend and savior one can ever have.

My hope is to hear Jesus say to me, "Well done, good and obedient servant. Enter into my kingdom."

To find out more about Howard Storm and his near-death experience, why not check out his other books:

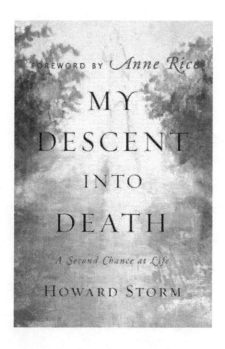

Not since Betty Eadie's Embraced by the Light has a personal account of a Near-Death Experience (NDE) been so utterly different from most others—or nearly as compelling.

"This is a book you devour from cover to cover, and pass on to others. This is a book you will quote in your daily conversation. Storm was meant to write it and we were meant to read it." – from the foreword by Anne Rice.

In the thirty years since Raymond Moody's Life After Life appeared, a familiar pattern of NDEs has emerged: suddenly floating over one's own body, usually in a hospital setting, then a sudden hurtling through a tunnel of light toward a presence of love. Not so in Howard Storm's case.

Storm, an avowed atheist, was awaiting emergency surgery when he realized that he was at death's door. Storm found himself out of his own body, looking down on the hospital room scene below. Next, rather than going "toward the light," he found himself being torturously dragged to excruciating realms of darkness and death, where he was physically assaulted by monstrous beings of evil. His description of his pure terror and torture is unnerving in its utter originality and convincing detail.

Finally, drawn away from death and transported to the realm of Heaven, Storm met angelic beings as well as the God of Creation. In this fascinating account, Storm tells of his "life review," his conversation with God, even answers to age-old questions such as why the Holocaust was allowed to take place. Storm was sent back to his body with a new knowledge of the purpose of life here on earth. This book is his message of hope.

https://howardstorm.com/books/

By Howard Storm

Made in the USA
Monee, IL
12 September 2024

65595540R00109